D0836789

Performing the Gospel

Performing the Gospel

Exploring the Borderland of Worship,
Entertainment, and the Arts

Deborah Sokolove

 CASCADE *Books* · Eugene, Oregon

PERFORMING THE GOSPEL
Exploring the Borderland of Worship, Entertainment, and the Arts

Copyright © 2019 Deborah Sokolove. All rights reserved. Except for brief quotations in critical publications or reviews, no part of this book may be reproduced in any manner without prior written permission from the publisher. Write: Permissions, Wipf and Stock Publishers, 199 W. 8th Ave., Suite 3, Eugene, OR 97401.

Cascade Books
An Imprint of Wipf and Stock Publishers
199 W. 8th Ave., Suite 3
Eugene, OR 97401

www.wipfandstock.com

PAPERBACK ISBN: 978-1-4982-9696-0
HARDCOVER ISBN: 978-1-4982-9698-4
EBOOK ISBN: 978-1-4982-9697-7

Cataloging-in-Publication data:

Names: Sokolove, Deborah, author.

Title: Performing the gospel : exploring the borderland of worship, entertainment, and the arts / by Deborah Sokolove.

Description: Eugene, OR : Cascade Books, 2019 | Includes bibliographical references and index.

Identifiers: ISBN 978-1-4982-9696-0 (paperback) | ISBN 978-1-4982-9698-4 (hardcover) | ISBN 978-1-4982-9697-7 (ebook)

Subjects: LCSH: Christianity and the arts. | Worship. | Liturgics.

Classification: LCC BR115.A8 S6 2019 (print) | LCC BR115.A8 (ebook)

Manufactured in the U.S.A.   MARCH 7, 2019

Scripture quotations are from New Revised Standard Version Bible, copyright 1989, Division of Christian Education of the National Council of the Churches of Christ in the United States of America. Used by permission. All rights reserved.

Contents

Acknowledgments

THERE ARE ALWAYS so many people to thank that it is certain I will leave out someone important. It is also difficult to know where to begin. Therefore, I will begin at the beginning, with Wesley Theological Seminary, which has been my professional home for nearly twenty-five years, and which gave me sabbatical time to write and think as I started this volume. In particular, I am grateful to President David McAllister-Wilson, for the trust he has put in me to lead the Center for the Arts and Religion; to Dean Bruce Birch, for his generous support and mentorship, and for understanding that the arts can lead theological education into places it might never otherwise find; to Amy Gray, associate director of the Center for the Arts and Religion, without whose organizational skills and creative problem-solving I would never feel free to leave the office; and to the staff of the library at Wesley Theological Seminary, who always answered my questions and found missing volumes with a smile, and their director, James Estes, who pointed me to important resources and helped me translate Middle English into something slightly more readable. I am grateful, also, to Robert Wright and Dean Scott Woodward of the Oblate School of Theology, who graciously arranged for me to spend a month as their guest as this book was just beginning to take form; to the staff of the Oblate Renewal Center, especially Sister Susan Marie Hazenski, SSCM, associate director, and Jenny Mattingsley, food director, who made sure that I had meals and coffee and wireless access and made me feel welcome and cared for, so that I could lose myself in reading and writing without worrying about the practicalities of life.

I also give thanks to all the artists and scholars who graciously gave me their time and thoughts as they sat in front of my camera or talked with me through the magic of digital media. They are, in alphabetical order: Roy Barber, Cláudio Carvalhaes, Ruth Duck, Heather Murray Elkins, Ken Fong, Eileen Guenther, Kim Harris, Marlita Hill, Heather Josselyn-Cranson,

ACKNOWLEDGMENTS

Gordon Lathrop, Tom Long, Marcia McFee, Mark Miller, Geoffrey Moore, Carl Petter Opsahl, Tracy Radosevic, Gail Ramshaw, Don Saliers, Melva Sampson, Lisa Cole Smith, and Janet Walton. I also recorded a part of a discussion about worship, performance, entertainment, and the arts with the Feminist Studies in Liturgy seminar at the North American Academy of Liturgy in January 2016, which helped inform my thinking. In addition to several persons already mentioned, participants included Kathy Black, Jill Crainshaw, Elizabeth Moore, Sylvia Sweeney, and Chelsea Yarborough. Without the enthusiastic support of everyone who shared their thoughts with me, it is certain that this book would not exist.

Thanks also to Kerric Harvey, who graciously provided me with her script for *The Interrogation Project*; to Matthew Wimer at Cascade Books, who gave me several reprieves when I was unable to complete the work in the time I had set aside to do it; and to my faculty colleagues, who were always ready to sympathize when the writing bogged down.

Finally, I am grateful to John Morris, my friend and editor, who read my early drafts with patience, helped me make sense of what seemed to be a hopeless mess, pointed out my errors, and is not responsible for those that remain; to my husband, Glen Yakushiji, who supports me in more ways than I can count; and to my grown-up children, who cheer me on from across the country and across the ocean. To everyone else who has helped me along the way, please accept my apologies for not naming you individually. You know who you are.

Introduction

PUBLIC, CORPORATE WORSHIP—ALSO KNOWN as liturgy—is the heart of the church. Whether we gather on Sunday mornings or on Wednesday evenings or at noon every day, worshipping the Triune God together on a regular basis is what distinguishes Christians from all the altruistic, humanitarian folk who do good works in the social, political, or personal arenas. As Heb 10:24–25 admonishes us, the way we are to "consider how to provoke one another to love and good deeds," is through "not neglecting to meet together, as is the habit of some, but encouraging one another" in fellowship and praising God. Other passages in the New Testament are just as clear about the primary place that regular, communal worship has in our spiritual and everyday lives. In Matt 18:20, Jesus promises to be present wherever two or three are gathered in his name. The end of the second chapter of the Acts of the Apostles praises the constancy of the three thousand new converts, who "devoted themselves to the apostles' teaching and fellowship, to the breaking of bread and the prayers."[1] Later in Acts, as Paul is about to leave Troas, gathering "on the first day of the week, when we met to break bread"[2] is understood as an established custom that is completely unremarkable. Similarly, 1 Cor 14 simply assumes that followers of Christ will gather frequently, each one bringing "a hymn, a lesson, a revelation, a tongue, or an interpretation," for building up the Body.

Despite such clear biblical mandates for regularly gathering with others for the worship of God, many people today claim to be Christian but rarely go to church. Many others reject Christianity outright, looking to other traditions for the spiritual nourishment that they do not find in Christianity; still others claim to be, as the saying goes, spiritual but not religious. As many studies and news articles have noted, the fastest growing

1. Acts 2:42.
2. Acts 20:7.

ix

religious demographic in the United States is those with no institutional affiliation.

Tradition, Worship, and Entertainment

While denominations lament their shrinking numbers and local congregations try, often unsuccessfully, to attract young families as they watch their existing members age, move away to retirement communities, become house-bound, or simply die, a few well-known churches have weekly attendance figures in the thousands. These mega-churches, as they are sometimes called, often have charismatic leaders, innovative approaches to worship, and a full slate of family-friendly services including infant care, book stores, coffee shops, and even sports facilities.

What the mega-churches do not have is what is often called the "traditional" style of worship that is prevalent in many denominational churches today. They do not have hymnals or prayer books, they do not read scripture according to the lectionary, and they may not even have a printed order of worship or bulletin. For those who find their spiritual home in a mega-church, this lack of tradition is precisely the point. Tradition, for them, equals boring.

I have attended a great many so-called traditional worship services at churches all over the United States, and a few in Europe and Asia. Some follow the worshipping pattern prescribed by one or another denominational tradition; others were shaped by the frontier revivals of the late nineteenth and early twentieth centuries; still others intentionally derive their local custom from two or more worshiping traditions, often because of recent mergers; and some others, like the emerging church movement, are trying to recover an ancient pattern of worship in a modern idiom. I have discovered that tradition means different things in different places. I can also understand, from what I have seen in some churches, the appeal of the mega-churches as well as that of staying home to read the Sunday papers, having a leisurely brunch with friends, or going for a hike in the woods. At too many churches, regardless of denomination, worship is a slipshod affair, with leaders slouching in with their hands in their pockets, mumbling inexpertly into microphones squealing with feedback, and delivering sermons that ramble off into local folklore or in-jokes that are incomprehensible to visitors. At such services, there is often no discernible connection between the scripture readings, the hymns, and the topic of the sermon, and no sense of awe regarding the living God who is nevertheless in their midst, though apparently unnoticed. At others, the choir sings with professional polish, readers and preachers are well-trained, and everything is so formal and decorous and nice that I find myself wondering if they would recognize Jesus if he walked in off the street.

Whether too casual or too uptight, for the many people who do not go to church regularly, what happens in these churches does not address their spiritual hungers. Faced with shrinking congregations and tightening budgets, many local churches are tempted to try to mimic the style of mega-churches with what they term a contemporary service, replacing choirs and organs with soloists wielding guitars and electric keyboards, and rejecting hymnals in favor of the projected words of recently composed praise choruses. Too often such congregations lack the resources to do this well. Outside of the larger metropolitan areas, where music instruction is relatively available, the praise bands that are intended to bring in younger people are too often not well trained, have a too narrow repertoire, and annoy the older members of the congregation by turning the sound up too loud. At least, that is the common story that I hear at conferences and around the seminary lunch table.

On the other hand, worship at a mega-church is never slipshod, never uptight, and never, ever boring. Instead, it is generally upbeat, with dramatic skits and music whose production values rival rock concerts or Broadway shows, and preachers whose presentation is as polished and engaging as a TED Talk. As a recent article on the ABC News website puts it, "Some congregations swell their ranks with the entertaining Sunday show, feel-good sermons, and an appealing social environment, instead of focusing on the core religious message."[3] In describing such worship as an entertaining show, it is clear that the author was not intending it as a compliment.

I find myself troubled by this recurrent conversation in church circles in which words like "entertainment" and "performance," as well as "boring" and "traditional," are used as weapons, hurled accusingly at various styles of preaching and worship that the speaker doesn't like or doesn't agree with. This book arises out of that discomfort, as I struggle to articulate what it is about performance and entertainment that arouses such passionate feelings and how we can find a way to talk about varying worship styles that is helpful rather than divisive.

3. Libaw, "More Americans," para. 39.

Part of my discomfort lies in the pejorative way that notions of performance are used to criticize certain kinds of worship, as though there is something wrong with performance as such. My father's family were all performers, professional musicians who grew up in both the klezmer and classical traditions. After spending his early teen summers touring the Catskills with my grandfather and an ever-changing number of his brothers as part of the Joseph Sokolove and Sons Klezmer Orchestra, my father became a studio musician, playing whatever music was required with whatever band or orchestra he was hired to play with. One of my treasured pieces of memorabilia is a photograph showing him in his chair as first violinist with the Peck Radio Hour orchestra, sometime in the 1930s. On the other side of my family, my mother's father designed some of the original sequin-spangled shirts worn by Hollywood cowboys. At least, that is what he told me when I used to visit his magical embroidery factory in the Los Angeles garment district. I myself made a few forays into the world of entertainment as a semi-professional folk dancer before I turned to the visual arts, and the focus of my MFA studies was in computer animation, another brand of entertainment, if not live performance. All of the artists I know, whether in my work at the Luce Center for the Arts and Religion at Wesley Theological Seminary or in my travels in the secular art world, are serious about their craft, whether their work is destined for the classical concert hall or local bar, the Shakespearean stage or the comedy club, the art museum or the church. Therefore, when people speak of "mere" entertainment, or say that something is "just" a performance, I often wonder why we call some forms of art serious and legitimate parts of life, and even invite them into our worship, while dismissing other styles or genres as worthless entertainment. Why are these words so problematic, and how can we reclaim the notions of expertise and enjoyment as legitimate parts of Christian worship?

Exploring the Borderland

This volume is neither an analysis of social trends in church attendance nor a critique of the larger issues surrounding the increasing reliance on electronic devices and social media in our lives. Nor is it an attempt to criticize either the small, local congregation that is trying to do its best with limited resources and growing needs; the more affluent, suburban congregation that expects the same level of professionalism in its worship as it does in other areas of life; or the large mega-church that draws crowds with well-produced, carefully planned presentations that sometimes look to some more theatrical than worshipful. All three approaches have deep roots in the history of Christ's church. And all three, along with their many variants, pose important questions about the relationship between Christian worship, entertainment, and the arts. What this volume proposes to do is to explore the territory where these questions lurk behind every decision.

Some of these questions include: What is the difference between good worship and good entertainment? Can something that is intended to be entertainment also be worshipful? What is performance and why does it matter? What is the difference between ritual, art, and entertainment? Is worship or ritual itself an art form? If so, who is the artist and who is the audience? How can the arts contribute to worship without taking over and turning it into *just* a performance? What is the appropriate role of artists in worship? How do we balance artistic excellence and congregational participation? Is there a line between worship and entertainment? If so, where is it, and how do we know when we have crossed it?

To help me answer these questions, I conducted twenty-one interviews with theater people, dancers, musicians, preachers, liturgical scholars, and those whose concerns and expertise cannot be confined to a single category. Some of the performing artists work primarily in the secular world while some work entirely within and for the church, and some do both. Some of those whom I have interviewed spend most of their time and energy serving a single, local congregation; some write and teach at seminaries and other places of learning; and others travel extensively to concert venues or church social halls or retreat centers or conventions, sharing their gifts wherever they are welcomed. Most are passionately engaged with the worship life of the Church Universal, and all have thought deeply about the questions at hand long before they allowed me to interview them for the sake of this book. With all of their voices brought together in a single volume, their individual ideas seem less like an argument than a conversation among people who all want to perform the Gospel in the best way that they can.

About This Book

In the chapters to follow, I will share what I heard in the interviews and what I have gleaned from the writings of others to attempt to address these and similar questions from a variety of perspectives. The first chapter offers a few stories that ask how we can tell whether any given event is worship or entertainment, ritual or art. Chapter 2 attempts to address the relationship between good worship and good entertainment by presenting the ideas of eleven of the people I interviewed. Most of this is in their own words, which are lightly edited, summarized, or paraphrased for clarity.

Chapter 3 begins with a rehearsal of the role of worship in pre-modern society and the development of what eventually became the modern theater, ending with a few examples of events that blur the lines between worship and entertainment today. While this is a fairly well-trodden path, the perspective taken in this chapter will suggest that we have been concentrating on only the main highway while ignoring other interesting and valuable roads.

Chapter 4 provides a few guideposts to the territory, defining some of the words that consistently lead to misunderstandings when people talk about worship, entertainment, and the arts. Performance, however, carries so much weight that it takes up all of chapter 5. Drawing on performance theory as well as more colloquial understandings of what performance means and its role in various areas of life, this chapter considers the roles that pretending, rehearsing, and other fictions play in everyday life and in Christian worship, exploring some of the issues that raise anxiety around performance in the church.

Chapter 6 returns to the interviews, presenting the thoughts of ten more liturgical experts as a way to reflect on what has been seen and heard in the preceding explorations. Finally, chapter 7 reviews where the conversation has gone, looks for resonances and tensions, and suggests some ways of moving forward with a little more clarity.

This book is written for my students, both the ones with whom I have already shared much of what I have written here, and those who I have yet to meet. It is my hope that as you explore the ritual/entertainment/performing-arts borderlands and listen to the voices of the people I interviewed and the voices of those whom I have only met through their words on a page or through the internet, and as you read my own reports from the field, you, too, will want to travel along some of the broad roads and narrow byways where the Body of Christ continually discovers new ways to perform the Gospel.

one

What Are We Doing Here?

A minister with whom I once worked used to explain church rituals to me like this: We do not do these things because we know exactly what they mean. We do them in order to find out what they mean.[1]

CAN SOMETHING THAT IS intended as entertainment also be worshipful? Can something that is intended to be worship also be entertaining? Sometimes, it is difficult to know what kind of event we are attending. We may think that we are going to church to pray with other members of a congregation, but once we get there it seems more like a concert or a play that we are expected to watch like members of an audience. Or, we may think that we are going to a play for an evening's entertainment, only to find ourselves overcome with a sense of the divine. What are we doing when we go to church, a concert, a play, or a movie?

Three Church Stories

Story one begins on a Sunday morning in Advent at a large church in an affluent neighborhood. The space was large and gracious, with high, white walls; large, arched, clear glass windows; blond wood pews; and a platform at the front featuring pulpit on the right, lectern at the left, organ in the back, and ample space for a large choir. I had been invited to give a slide

1. Paulsell, "Writing," 24.

1

talk for the adult Sunday school, and, as is my custom in such cases, had stayed to worship with the community. As I entered the nave, I was somewhat surprised to see the entire platform filled with risers, and the space immediately below it set with enough folding chairs and music stands for a small orchestra.

By the time the service was about to start, every pew was filled with festively attired, mostly White families and a sense of excited expectation hung in the air. Soon, a robed choir, four soloists dressed as if for a concert, and a group of dark-suited musicians carrying instruments filed in and took their places. While the proceedings were framed as worship, the prayers were perfunctory, and the sermon did little more than recount the history of Christmas cantatas in this congregation and introduce the guest soloists and conductor. The well-designed bulletin bore more than a passing resemblance to a concert program with its performance notes, photos, and bios of the professional soloists, who were not members of the congregation.

Clearly, much effort and expense had gone into producing the excellent performance of the "Coming of the Messiah" section of Handel's *Messiah* that those attending expected to experience. Equally clearly, by the time of the closing benediction, many of those present felt that they had worshipped God that morning, uplifted by the magnificent music into direct contemplation of the divine. I, however, missed the opportunity for meaningful congregational participation in confession, thanksgiving, petition, and intercession that has been a hallmark of Christian worship since the earliest times. I wondered how this aesthetic experience differed from similar musical performances held in concert halls for audiences who rarely attend any church.

Story two begins on a Saturday evening, once again in Advent. This event was held at a church that was architecturally similar to the first, and, like the first, was in an affluent neighborhood. Also like the first, it included a large choir. However, this time the members of the church were supplemented not by paid vocalists but by highly skilled volunteers from the surrounding community. The small orchestra was drawn both from the ranks of the congregation and from the teachers and students of the music conservatory housed in the church building. The musical program was titled *Light in Deepest Night* and advertised as "an Advent Concert in remembrance of the victims of gun violence and in hope for a more peaceful world." Both performers and audience were racially diverse. The event included a freewill offering to benefit a scholarship in honor of Rev.

Clementa Pinckney, who had been murdered the previous summer while at prayer in his church in Charleston, South Carolina. The program notes explain:

> Light in Deepest Night was originally written as a Lenten *meditatio* based on the writing of Julian of Norwich. Aaron David Miller is the original composer. David L. Miller is the original librettist. The work has been modified for Advent and to remember the victims of gun violence and to express hope for a more peaceful world with new orchestration by [the conductor] and a new compilation of meditations by [members of the church pastoral staff].[2]

In addition to the specially composed orchestral and choral pieces, the program included readings of poems by Evelyn Scott, Langston Hughes, Christian Wiman, Jane Kenyon, Wendell Berry, Maya Angelou, Laura Martin, and Walt Whitman; selections from the Hebrew and Christian scriptures, the Koran, and the Department of Parish Development of the Presbyterian Church of New Zealand; and a poetic prayer identified as written by an eighth-century Indian Buddhist named Shantideva. Interspersed among all of these were some reflections on gun violence in general, statistics about the ways gun violence affects various communities, a list of many who had died in mass shootings in the past year, and some personal memories offered by members of the pastoral staff of young people who had been killed by guns. In addition to all of this, the audience was invited to sing four traditional Advent hymns along with the choir and orchestra.

In his introductory remarks to the program, the pastor asked the audience not to clap between numbers, explaining that the intention was for the entire evening to be understood as a cohesive whole, beginning with gloomy, monochrome darkness and moving towards a joyous dawn. The program ended with a benediction, recessional, and closing hymn, after which everyone was finally invited to applaud.

At the reception in the social hall, I heard people talking about the excellence of the performers, particularly one singer who was probably in her young teens. The emotions that seemed to be expressed more than any others were appreciation of the church's overall commitment to good music and approbation of its commitment to the cause of racial reconciliation. Of course, not everyone finds it easy to talk about deeply felt emotional responses, so what I heard may have simply been initial, polite conversation. Just as I had wondered whether the performance of *Messiah* was worship or

2 Westmoreland, "Light," 2.

high-class entertainment, now I wondered whether what had been billed as a concert was really a Christian worship service in disguise. Was it a concert or worship? Or was it something that exists in an intermediate space, neither strictly speaking a religious event nor an evening's entertainment, but somehow exhibiting elements of both?

The third story occurred the next morning, within the ordinary, Sunday morning worship of a small, nondenominational, progressive Christian congregation.[3] In this much smaller, but still gracious, worship space, chairs, altar,[4] and lectern all stood at the same level on the glowing, hardwood floor, the light pouring through clear glass windows punctuating pale blue walls. Everything was simple, lovingly handmade by skilled, creative craftspeople.

At the time reserved for the sermon within the regular order of worship, six members of the congregation came forward to offer a group testimony, *Guns: From Despair to Hope.* The participants were all members of a small group that meets together weekly to support one another in their individual spiritual journeys, and to seek opportunities for prayer and action in response to the many places in the world that are in need of justice, peace, and healing. One by one, they stood not behind the lectern, but in front of the altar and the cross, telling stories of having guns, hating guns, fearing guns, using guns, having guns turned against them. When all the stories were told, one member of the group named aloud forty-three people who had been killed with guns, some famous, others unknown to most of the congregation. As she read the names, the other members of the group did a slow, silent dance expressing their individual reactions. After the last name, the reader began to sing a wordless chant in the Jewish prayer tradition known as *niggun,* starting slowly and mournfully and gradually building into a joyous dance into which she invited the entire congregation.[5]

3. This, as it happens, is my own congregation, but I believe I can tell the story without bias. The reader of course, must be the judge.

4. In Roman Catholic, Orthodox, and some other denominations, the place where Eucharist is celebrated is called the altar, seeing it as the place where Christ continually offers himself in the broken bread and wine poured out as his body and blood. Many Protestants call it a table since their theologies insist that sacrifice is not involved in the ritual commemoration of Christ's life, death, and resurrection. Others refer to this piece of liturgical furniture as the altar-table, joining both the sacrificial and the meal aspects of the celebration. However, in this volume I will follow the colloquial usage and simply call it the altar regardless of denominational or theological distinctions.

5. The text of the testimonies may be found at http://www.seekerschurch.dream-hosters.com/worship/sermons/1627-gun-violence-despair-to-hope-by-he-eyes-to-

In some ways, what happened on that Sunday morning was similar to the concert the night before. Both were held in Christian churches where the congregation is committed to peace and justice. Both involved personal testimony, a reading of a list of victims, and music. However, there the resemblance ends. The Saturday evening event was very reserved, precise, aesthetically very pleasing yet somehow distancing. The music was beautiful and beautifully performed. And in that very well-rehearsed perfection, it seemed to me that the passion the musicians, speakers, and even the audience felt was subsumed into the artistry. Like the performance of *Messiah*, it was an event designed to evoke an aesthetic experience, to inspire refined appreciation rather than to experience the immediacy of raw emotions. The recitation of facts and statistics allowed the largely affluent, educated, suburban audience to feel safe even as the subject was violence and death. There was only one point at which it seemed that real emotion broke through, as one of the speakers recounted the life and death of a young man whom she had known and befriended at another church. Even so, it seemed to me that her well-rehearsed poise and the physical remove imposed by her station in the pulpit distanced her from the audience several feet below. Still, given how much money was raised for the benefit of seminarians who might follow in the footsteps of the martyred pastor in whose memory the event was held, I am certain that many were touched, however blurred the lines between entertainment and worship.

The Sunday morning event, on the other hand, was raw, immediate, and difficult. The presenters were people well known in the relatively small congregation. They were on the same flat floor as the people seated in chairs only a few feet away, not on an elevated stage. By the end of the second person's story, I could feel myself shaking with emotion, hoping it would end soon and hoping it would never end. When it finally did, the congregation sat in stunned silence, unable to move or speak for what seemed like a very long time. In the reflections that followed, when someone wondered aloud whether this performance might be done again for a wider audience, the participants looked shocked, shaking their heads in a definitive "no." This was meant to be intimate, to be shared only in the safety of a place where they were known and loved, not to be put on display for strangers. It was meant to make the danger of both gun violence and of the Divine palpably present to everyone there. There was no question that what we had experienced was the Gospel, proclaimed and performed in our midst.

see-ears-to-hear-peace-prayer-mission-group.

A Play

As I was pondering these three examples of the blurry borderland between worship and entertainment, I attended a play that explored that borderland in a very different way. Clearly intended as performance rather than worship, Kerric Harvey's *The Interrogation Project* was billed as an "ethnographic experiment" exploring "the ethics of torture in the terrorist era, focusing especially on race and gender."[6] Held in a university classroom, it addressed the use of violence for the purpose of getting information from prisoners in times of war, with both presenters and audience from varied and often indeterminate ethnic backgrounds. Using elements usually associated with initiation rituals rather than entertainment, the audience members were invited into a receptive mood by first assembling in a room separate from that of the performance. When everyone who had made reservations had arrived, the audience was ushered together as a group into a darkened theater lit only by candles, where it was announced that the door would be locked so that no one could enter or leave until the performance was over.

Loosely set in the American South a few years before the Civil War, the short play depicts members of the Underground Railroad who are attempting to uncover a traitor in their midst. Using simple props and minimal costuming to evoke an "anyplace," it features Grace, an African-American woman who is the leader of the interrogation team; Billy, Grace's subordinate; and Viktor, the person being interrogated. The play was presented three times in succession, with only the casting of the two men changing from one version to the next. In the first version, both men are White; in the second version, the one being interrogated appears to be Middle Eastern and the interrogator/torturer is White; and in the third, these two roles are reversed. As the violence escalates, the dialogue reveals each of the interrogators' struggle to reconcile their sense of the rightness of their cause with their inhumane treatment of their captive.

Between the three stagings of the play, the house lights remained dim and the audience was instructed to be silent, deepening the sense of ritual and mystery. Following the third "act," the house lights came on and the cast came on stage as themselves to take their bows to somewhat muted applause, as the audience seemed to struggle to return to a more rational, discursive consciousness. In the discussion that followed, it became clear

6. Harvey, "Interrogation," flyer.

that as the racial/ethnic dynamic between the two men and between each of them and the woman changed from one version to another, the audience's ability to empathize with the various characters changed. So did their understanding of the time and place of the play. Were we in the American South in 1858? Was it Afghanistan or Syria or Guantanamo in 2016? Or was the setting simply some place outside of ordinary time and space, in which these questions continue to echo eternally?

What was equally clear was that the audience actively avoided any mention of the ritual quality of the event. No one mentioned the candles, the silence, or the effect of the locked doors, all of which reminded me of ancient baptismal rituals. The discussion quickly turned to the scholarly and analytic, as if the sense of participatory involvement that Harvey had worked so hard to create was too uncomfortable to even address once the lights came on. While clearly not worship, it was not clear if this event was art, ritual, or some odd, transformative amalgam of the two.

Who or What do We Entertain?

Reflecting on these stories, it is clear that many kinds of gatherings cannot simply be put into a single category. In a recent discussion at the North American Academy of Liturgy, Heather Murray Elkins reframed the definition of entertainment by asking, "What do we entertain?" Elkins reminded those present that "to entertain" can also mean "to pay attention to." She asked, What thoughts or ideas do we entertain? Who or what do we give attention or consideration to? Are we paying attention to the people and things that really matter, or are we distracting ourselves? Are we avoiding the real questions, the ones that will lead us to transformative actions?

This book is an attempt to look at some of the ways that performing artists, liturgical scholars, preachers, and people who care about public, corporate Christian worship address these questions. It is an exploration of what I am increasingly coming to call a borderland, a broad, not-entirely-explored place where ritual, entertainment, and the arts meet and separate and overlap along the highways and alleyways of life. In the next chapter, we will enter that borderland and listen as some of those who serve as guides explain which signposts seem to point toward worship, which to entertainment, and which lead us into a deeper place that is neither and both.

two

Is Good Worship Good Entertainment?

Thus I fluctuate between peril of pleasure and approved wholesomeness;
inclined the rather (though not as pronouncing an irrevocable opinion)
to approve of the usage of singing in the church; that so by the delight of
the ears the weaker minds may rise to the feeling of devotion. Yet when
it befalls me to be more moved with the voice than the words sung, I
confess to have sinned penally, and then had rather not hear music.[1]

EVERYBODY HAS AN OPINION on what constitutes good entertainment. Some
people like the broad humor of situation comedies, while others prefer the
more cerebral humor of Jon Stewart, and still others would rather watch
football or go to the circus. Likewise, everybody who cares about church at
all (and even many who don't) has an opinion about good worship. Some
people prefer the austere silence of a Quaker meeting or the quiet, repetitive chants of Taizé. Others are drawn to the enthusiastic singing and clapping of a gospel choir in a Pentecostal church. Still others are not satisfied
with anything except three hymns and a good, solid Presbyterian sermon.

Regardless of their preferences, it is not unusual for people to talk
about entertainment in religious or spiritual terms. Likewise, worship services are often judged on criteria that might be better suited to a concert
or a play. While worship that is boring will eventually drive away even

1. Augustine, *Confessions*, 10.33, 190.

8

the most committed of Christians, does it follow that worship should be entertaining?

To begin my exploration of the borderland where worship and entertainment come together, I interviewed many experts who care deeply about worship, entertainment, or both. Each interview began with the question "In your opinion, what is the difference between good worship and good entertainment?" followed by a free-form conversation elaborating the initial response. Each interview lasted from thirty minutes to a full hour. The answers ranged from confident assertions that there is no difference to equally clear insistence that the one has nothing to do with the other. Other replies questioned the premise, offered differing understandings of worship, entertainment, art, or performance, or suggested ways of thinking about what "good" might mean in the context of worship, entertainment, or both.

Gail Ramshaw: The Baptized Community

Gail Ramshaw is a retired professor of religion who studies and crafts liturgical language from her home outside of Washington, DC. Her many publications include *Treasures Old and New: Images in the Lectionary* and *The Three-Day Feast: Maundy Thursday, Good Friday, and Easter*. She currently serves as an editorial consultant for the journals *Worship* and *Studia Liturgica*.

A scholar and teacher with deep Lutheran roots and a great love of the liturgy as it has changed to nourish Christians through the past two millennia, Ramshaw sent a brief letter in response to the question about worship and entertainment, defining worship as "the ritual through which the baptized community renders prayer and praise to God." Likening worship more to a group singing "Happy Birthday" to a friend than an audience attending the symphony, Ramshaw notes that although worship may include choral and instrumental music as well as other ritual actions that might be thought of as entertainment in another venue, "applause is not usually welcomed, since that might suggest our appreciation of a performance of some piece of entertainment." Defining entertainment as "something presented to an audience for their pleasure," Ramshaw continues:

> Worship as entertainment is nothing new: an example is a medieval high mass, elaborately conducted by elegantly robed experts before a silent audience. Of the revival at Cane Ridge, it was said

that more souls were begot than saved: the event was in large part prairie entertainment.[2]

Ramshaw goes on to lament the way in which worship often becomes confused with entertainment:

> Because our society offers free nonstop entertainment, and our populace has become accustomed to having entertainment frame everything from political debate to funerals, it is difficult for Christian assemblies to maintain worship as a participatory collaboration presented to God. My denomination has discouraged practices in which others worship for us. Here's one example: we have come to title organists and choir directors as "leaders of assembly song," the focus not on individual talent but on communal activity. I pity those congregations that are captive to the lures of entertainment: how in the world do they choose what will entertain a diverse group of people, who are bonded only by their baptism and faith in Christ's resurrection? It seems to me that the greater the role of entertainment in worship, the narrower will be the demographics of the assembly, and the more passive its conduct.[3]

It is clear that for Ramshaw, the word "entertainment" has certain negative overtones, and as such has no place in a service of Christian worship. It is not that she is against pleasure, nor does she disagree that there is a place for laughter and enjoyment, even in worship. Rather, for Ramshaw, entertainment suggests a kind of performance in which some participants put on a show, while an audience enjoys what is presented. Christian worship, on the other hand, is the gathered congregation singing, praying, and keeping silence together as they remember their baptism and practice becoming the Body of Christ.

Gordon Lathrop: Audiences and Congregations

Gordon W. Lathrop is professor of liturgy emeritus at the Lutheran Theological Seminary in Philadelphia. A pastor of the Evangelical Lutheran Church in America, he is the author of several books, has lectured widely in several countries, and has participated in the work of the Faith and Order

2. Ramshaw, letter, 2015.
3. Ramshaw, letter, 2015.

Commission of the World Council of Churches and the Worship and Culture Study of the Lutheran World Federation.

Lathrop acknowledges that profound things can be communicated in what sometimes is called entertainment. However, he prefers to begin with the distinction between audience and congregation. Christian worship, he insists, must

> be marked by congregations, assemblies that are engaged or practicing. And the performance of the arts for the sake of entertainment, that has got to be marked by an audience. Congregation and audience are not the same things. Theologically, the congregation is going to be marked by its assembly as the Body of Christ, by its baptismal identity. An audience is not marked by its baptismal identity. It is marked by its interest in the performer.[4]

This is not to say that performance is absent in the Christian assembly. Those who lead worship are, of necessity, performing in the sense that they are doing something that requires practice and presence. However, Lathrop notes that the liturgical and theological critique about their performance has to do with the appropriate exercise of power in a way that does not happen at a concert or other entertainment. In worship, the question is, How is the community served by the power of the leaders? This is less of a question in a concert, where service to the community is not usually an issue.

There are, of course, ways in which worship and entertainment overlap. Lathrop is clear about this:

> In liturgy, I am interested in having a rehearsal. I am really interested in readers who can read well, choirs that can sing well, musicians that can play their music well. I'm interested in going to a room for worship that is going to be marked by architectural excellence and by some artists who have done work that really accords with what the Christian assembly is trying to do. But there is a difference. The question will be service. The best presider is the presider who understands that presiding is done by serving. The best musicians are going to be musicians who know that the best way that music works in Christian liturgy is as the leadership of assembly with song, not as performance of virtuoso numbers. The reader will read excellently, but not in such a way as to call attention to herself about her amazing dramatic skills.[5]

---

4. Lathrop, interview, 2015.
5. Lathrop, interview, 2015.

Lathrop also notes that there is a particular danger in the kind of buildings used for Christian worship that look like proscenium stages. These buildings encourage the congregation to think of itself as an audience seated in an auditorium or concert hall, with the actors up front. An audience is relatively passive, yielding to the power of the performer. A congregation, on the other hand, comes to participate and to be transformed through the ritual that is Christian worship.

This ritual, or liturgy, is different from a play, but in some circumstances, it can seem like one. Lathrop says that in a play, the actors are acting:

> The truth of the script is hidden. That is how it is entertainment. It is the principle that it is hidden. We discover the script as we go through it. The script of Christian liturgy is not hidden, or ought not be. I think we miss the boat there, sometimes, too. The script for Christian liturgy is communal property. We know what we are going to do when we do it. We are not acting. We are not pretending. We are doing something right now.[6]

At certain points in history, however, the liturgy stopped being communal property, and the congregation became an audience watching the leaders perform. In the Middle Ages, people did not gather around the table; they came to see the elaborately robed clergy enact what came to be called "ocular communion." Similarly, Lathrop notes, the revival meetings at Cane Ridge in the Second Great Awakening of the early nineteenth century became the best entertainment around, with great preaching and outpourings of the Spirit that were fun to watch. For Lathrop, however, what is most interesting about this particular moment is that

> the Second Great Awakening revival meetings started on the model from Scotland to be a preparation to go to Communion. You were supposed to repent listening to the preacher, see a preacher and confess your sins and your faith, and be given a token so you could go to the meeting house and go to Communion. I think that was a bad way to set up going to Communion, and I think it was on the whole not a very healthy way to do preaching and liturgy. I similarly think the late medieval Mass was not participatory. Certainly the Baroque buildings, where everything was focused on seeing, was malformed liturgy.[7]

6. Lathrop, interview, 2015.
7. Lathrop, interview, 2015.

Lathrop says that one of the ways we malform our churches today is to make them resemble places of entertainment, turning congregations into audiences. For him, good music, drama, and other performing arts are an important part of human life. Sometimes, they may even work as ritual, as when audience members follow the score of a beloved symphony, quietly recite from memory their favorite speeches in one of Shakespeare's plays, or sing along with the band at a rock concert. Nevertheless, none of these are Christian worship because they are not anchored in the identity of Jesus Christ.

Janet Walton: Performing Embodied Worship

Janet Walton recently retired as professor of worship at Union Theological Seminary in New York City. She is a past president of the North American Academy of Liturgy (1995–97), a Henry Luce Fellow in Theology and the Arts (1998), the recipient of a Henry Luce travel/research grant (1988), the 2003 recipient of the AAR Excellence in Teaching award, and the 2009 recipient of the Berakah Award, a lifetime award for distinctive work in worship given by the North American Academy of Liturgy.

Walton has been teaching and thinking about the relationship of worship and entertainment for many years. She responded to my question about worship and entertainment as follows:

> I think that my interest in entertainment as it relates to worship is not so much to discern whether it is entertainment or worship, but rather to say, What can these actions lead a community to do? I use peacock feathers, as I did at the Academy one year, to engender playfulness of people who are not playful, and then the next day in worship I found them ready to do things that they would not have done otherwise. I do not think of entertainment and worship as a sequence, or as this or that. I think about actions that some people may call entertainment, but I have in my mind that they lead a community to find their own voices, to free up their voices. And so sometimes I will do things like put on red clown noses, or have a fire dancer, or have an aerial dancer, and then they have very prescribed roles and some people may say this is entertainment.[8]

Walton believes that worship should gladden the heart, free the spirit, or bring people to a kind of openness, and that entertainment should be

8. Walton, interview, 2016.

a serious and important component of every worship service. Serious, however, does not mean humorless. She recalls a time when it was raining. When the organist played "Raindrops Keep Falling on my Head" as the prelude, everyone smiled. This sense that worship is broad and deep enough to include utter joy, profound sorrow, or anything in between informs Walton's definitions of both worship and performance:

> Entertainment may mean, Are we getting to you? Are we able to do something that really makes a step toward you instead of distancing from you? When I think of the word "performance," we have a lot of difficulty with our students because they think about superficial aspects of it, and of course the money aspects of it. But I feel like our communal responsibility to each other is to perform with each other and to invite each other into the performance. I cannot imagine using other words, because basically we want people to feel what the experience is from the tip of their toes to the top of their head.[9]

Performance, then, is embodied in everyone who is present:

> I think that is why the word performance is important and why it is so frightening to some, because our body is not necessarily under our cognitive control. Something happens and we are full of tears and there is nothing we can do to talk ourselves out of it. Or not much. And the same with joy. If you feel the joy, why, you just want to embrace people and thank God and thank one another. I am committed to the word "performance," but not in any superficial way. I do not think it is a superficial word. I think it is actually a very profound word.[10]

Walton's insistence on the importance of performance and embodiment led her to introduce the students in her Art and Worship class to the Blue Man Group, a performance art company which uses mime, dance, acrobatics, and other physical techniques in extraordinary ways. When she would take her students to the group's studio for a workshop, they did not immediately connect what they were doing in the workshop with worship. The Blue Man Group, Walton says,

> do not want to ever say a word, so they depend completely on their bodies. They told us what kind of discipline it takes to be able to communicate to each other and to the audience simply

9. Walton, interview, 2016.

10. Walton, interview, 2016.

with their bodies. And how difficult it is to work that way, and yet they have been communicating for twenty-five years, doing this show every night. When I take students down there, they pull out of our bodies what we did not know we had in our bodies because we cannot communicate with anything else—no words allowed. I bring them there because I feel like there is no baggage. The Blue Men have a commitment to imagination, to honor what a human being can do, which is far more than the straight go-into-the-pew-and-sit-down.[11]

Walton also took her students to a mask maker. After looking at the masks, they were able to try their own hands at it, in order to get a sense of the enormous possibilities of the human face. At other times, Walton would take students to museums, theaters, and other arts venues, in order to open more creative possibilities in their worship planning.

Because of her reputation for orchestrating innovative, rule-breaking worship services, Walton is often asked if these events are performances or worship. Refusing to see any contradiction, she replies:

I say, yes, for me, yes, it is a performance. It is a performance of a congregation for each other. It is a performance for the leaders with us. It is a performance of faith. And what we are really doing is putting it out there for one another to be able to engender another person's participation. It is meant to get to a place inside ourselves that maybe we have not touched before. Or maybe we have resisted before. I believe that worship without entertainment maybe would not work so well.[12]

Walton's assertion of the importance of entertainment as a component of worship is unusual, but not unique. Like Tracy Radosevic, whose comments follow, she argues for a more embodied understanding of Christian worship, to which we are not only free but encouraged to bring our whole selves, including our laughter and our tears, our fears as well as our hopes and prayers.

Tracy Radosevic: Stories that Draw Us In

Tracy Radosevic is an adjunct instructor at Wesley Theological Seminary, where she teaches biblical storytelling. She is a dynamic, energetic,

11. Walton, interview, 2016.
12. Walton, interview, 2016.

internationally acclaimed storyteller, educator, and retreat facilitator. Since 1991 she has traveled all over the United States, as well as to several foreign countries, bringing her special brand of humor, insight, and faith to audiences of all ages through the power of narrative.

At the other end of the conceptual spectrum from Gail Ramshaw, Radosevic is unwilling to make a distinction between good entertainment and good worship. She begins by defining entertainment:

> I'm a big lover of etymology. The etymology of the word "entertain" simply means to draw in, so how I'm defining it is "anything that draws the audience or congregation into an experience." I think entertainment has gotten a bad rap in some church circles— and rightly so, by the way!—because of what has been used to draw people in. You may have this great production value and lots of attention-getting bells and whistles but when it's all said and done, is there any real depth there? Often, the "show" ends up being more like cotton candy with no real nutritional value. In that case, I am *not* a supporter of entertaining worship! But if we are going with the original etymological understanding of the word "entertain," then my answer to your original question, "What's the difference between good entertainment and good worship?" would be "there's no difference." If your worship is constructed with integrity and in a way that draws people into an experience of and encounter with God, then that's entertainment. And in a worship context, it's entertainment in the best sense of the word.[13]

For her, worship is intended to draw people into the divine mystery, and the question is not whether or not it is entertainment, but whether it is done with the kind of integrity that she envisions. Radosevic acknowledges that, in many places, entertaining worship is not always done with integrity. Even when there are good intentions, too often there isn't enough time or the right kind of expertise or sufficient resources to allow for doing things well. Nonetheless, she insists, good worship is, or should be, good entertainment.

Returning to definitions, Radosevic points out that the word "perform" means "to render fully formed." Referring to a colleague's sarcastic reply to those who object to the notion of performance in worship, she notes that without performance, a worship service would be unformed, rendered only "half baked." Perhaps, she says, worship leaders need to reclaim the original

---

13. Radosevic, interview, 2015.

understandings of both entertainment and performance as a way to talk about what people do and experience in a service of Christian worship.

For Radosevic the hope would be that any such conversation would ultimately lead back to our Christian origins, where the performing of our stories of faith was central to the gathered community's experience. She says that stories are at the heart of relationships, and the biblical stories are at the heart of Christian worship. While she does not want to separate entertainment from worship, Radosevic does make a clear distinction between biblical storytelling and other forms of drama. Some of that comes down to personal storytelling style:

> I see storytelling as a long spectrum. And at one end of the spectrum would be my style of storytelling, which happens to have a lot of overlap with drama because I am naturally a more dramatic person. I have a more dramatic personality, so my style of storytelling is way down at the dramatic end of the storytelling spectrum. . . . Some of my favorite storytellers, however, are the ones whose style, even though they are up on stage performing, is much more down at the other end of the spectrum. They might be sitting on stage in a chair as they are telling, making only a few, small gestures. You wouldn't look at that and say, Wow, drama![14]

Moving from personal style to more theoretical concerns, Radosevic thinks that one of the biggest differences between storytelling and theatrical drama has to do with eye-contact and relationship with the audience. While there are always exceptions to the rule, in the theater the actors work behind an invisible fourth wall, acting as if the audience were not watching them. Because of this, the audience remain third-party observers. Even if they are deeply moved, there is never really an invitation to enter into what is going on because eye contact is not being made. Instead, most of the impact on the audience is created by the energy generated between the actors on the stage as they interact with one another. Conversely, Radosevic explains,

> with storytelling, it is the exact opposite. Making eye contact is imperative because you are relying on the audience to co-create the story with you. I, as the storyteller, am putting something out there and, with my eye contact, inviting you in so that you become actual characters in the story. You respond with laughs or grunts or snorts or whatever. I have to be picking up on the signals that

14. Radosevic, interview, 2015.

17

you are sending back, and I continue to change how I communicate based on the feedback provided by the audience.[15]

In storytelling, the energy is created through relationship between the storyteller and the audience. Even when the storyteller temporarily inhabits one or another character, it is still just the one person in front of the audience, as the audience takes the place of the other characters. This is true whether the storytelling happens in the context of a worship service or as a part of a festival or a standalone event. For Radosevic, performing is worship wherever it occurs:

> When I perform outside of worship, in some respects it is worship. I tell biblical stories in my bare feet as a sign of reverence. Different groups of people have different ways of showing that, covering their head, uncovering their head, genuflecting, crossing themselves, etc. I base my show of reverence on the story of Moses and the burning bush, and I do believe that when we enter into that time of sharing our sacred stories it is a sacred, holy place that we are entering.[16]

Radosevic calls this both entertainment and worship, in which she draws people into the Word of God. Indeed, even secular movies, which for many are the prime exemplar of entertainment, can be vehicles for noticing God's presence in the world. Radosevic and a colleague produce a podcast about movies people of faith should see, called "Faith and Focus." Discussing it, she notes,

> we almost always choose movies that you would not consider religious movies. We do that for a reason. We want to encourage people of faith to *always* be experiencing movies and life through the lens of faith. I never cease to be amazed at how often non-religious movies seem to have something to say about the journey of faith, if only our eyes are open to see it and our hearts open to receive it. Now is there something that *Shawshank Redemption* can teach us? Is there something in watching *Weekend at Bernie's* or Anna Deavere Smith through the lens of faith, is there something there that can provide instruction, challenge, a cautionary tale even, for our spiritual lives? I don't go to the movies necessarily to

---

15. Radosevic, interview, 2015.
16. Radosevic, interview, 2015.

feed my soul or to worship, but I think we'd be surprised at how often maybe they could.[17]

For Radosevic, a worship service can—and perhaps should—be entertaining, and even a silly movie might drop us right into the presence of God.

Melva L. Sampson: Storytelling as Sacred Performance

It is not just Radosevic who struggles with how to distinguish between performance and worship. Melva L. Sampson is assistant professor of preaching and practical theology at Wake Forest University School of Divinity. A practical theologian and ordained minister, her research interests include Black preaching, women's embodiment, African heritage spiritual traditions, Black girls' ritual performance, and the relationship between digital proclamation and spiritual formation. She is the creator and curator of *Pink Robe Chronicles* and *Raising Womanish Girls*, both digital platforms used to elucidate the role of sacred memory and ritual in the collective healing of marginalized communities.

Sampson speaks of storytelling as a sacred performance. In many African traditions, she points out, people are either born into a family of storytellers or individually called to be a *griot* or *jeli*.[18] Either way, they are taught how to tell the story, how to move in certain ways, when to pause, when to speak loudly or softly, and how to develop their own, authentic voice. Similarly, she says, many preachers in the African-American tradition learn how to move and speak with a certain musicality in order to help their congregations follow the sermon. Sampson suggests that this learning is an additional sense, like the sense of balance that anthropologist Kathryn Geurts describes in her discussion of the Anlo-Ewe people in Anlo-Land, Ghana.[19] Sampson explains:

> Geurts says that there is a sixth sense for this people. That sixth sense is balance. From childhood these people teach their children how to balance, sometimes literally balancing things on their head. Once they begin to master this balance of the head, then

17. Radosevic, interview, 2015.

18. Sampson uses both *griot* and *jeli* to refer to traditional West African storytellers who use song as well as story to preserve the oral traditions, genealogies, and historical narratives of their people.

19. Geurts, *Culture and the Senses*, 73–84.

balance begins to be embodied in how they carry themselves, how they walk. And not only does it come out in how they walk, it also comes out in their moral character. So, alongside the five senses, she would say there are things we can learn from different cultures when we consider that there is another kind of sensing. I would say that the musicality of Black preaching is a type of sensing, because it is something for those who are trained in this way from oral tradition.[20]

Sampson argues that the way of telling stories that was handed down through the oral tradition in Africa continues to inform preaching in the African-American church today:

> Uncle Sparky and Aunt Tammy, who are always lively at the family dinner or at Thanksgiving dinner with their storytelling antics, who we know are going to tell the stories, are also, in a way, preachers, and you are also learning this art of storytelling from them. That becomes a type of sensing, an embodied way to gather information and to disseminate information. I would say it comes from these indigenous traditions that were not destroyed in the transmission across the Atlantic to the States, but only submerged.[21]

While any individual preacher might have a hard time claiming to be a *griot* or *jeli* in the original sense of these terms, there is a style of preaching that can be traced to that tradition. As Sampson points out, this is not true just for those whose ancestors came from Africa. Rather, the underlying communicative patterns of any group necessarily shape how the stories of that group are told, whether at the dinner table, on the stage, or in church.

Don Saliers: Saturday Night and Sunday Morning

Don E. Saliers is William R. Cannon Distinguished Professor of Theology and Worship, Emeritus at Emory University's Candler School of Theology, where he currently serves as theologian-in-residence. An accomplished musician, theologian, scholar of liturgics, and a United Methodist pastor, Saliers has written numerous books and articles about worship and the arts that have influenced countless seminary students and pastors. His interest in the relationship between worship and entertainment led him to

20. Sampson, interview, 2016.
21. Sampson, interview, 2016.

co-author *A Song to Sing, a Life to Live* with his daughter, singer-songwriter Emily Saliers, one half of the popular folk-rock duo The Indigo Girls. Early in that book, Emily Saliers writes:

> I have felt the intensity of sacred music not only in the hallowed halls of church but also in the smoky bars of Atlanta, where all the "freaky people" . . . gather night after night to sing together, prop each other up through tragedy and joy, and cry an implicit prayer with their hearts. One place smells of incense and candles, the other of cigarette smoke and beer. I cannot say one experience is more deeply spiritual than the other.[22]

Musing on the ways that Saturday night can morph into Sunday morning, and how those two days and those two ways are not as separate as the question might imply, Don Saliers responded by making a connection with two other distinctions which he named as "sacred/secular" and "sacred/profane." Saliers makes it clear that he does not equate the secular with the profane:

> If something is profaned, it can be done in the name of God. Something is profane means that it is dehumanized, it is relegated to meaninglessness. Or it is, in fact, inverted from its original purpose for being. To profane a person is an incredibly ugly and dehumanizing act.[23]

Secular, on the other hand, refers to the world outside the church. In the Catholic tradition, he notes, a priest who does not belong to a religious order but rather is based in a particular diocese is called a "secular priest"—one who lives in the world rather than in a monastery. Reviewing the history of Christian music in the US, Saliers points to the notion of moral purity as it was expressed in the early twentieth century Pentecostal movement, which looked with particular suspicion on secular music. While some part of the early church rejected music outright, the Pentecostalists prohibited the use of certain instruments in worship because they were connected with dancing:

> The most interesting case for me now is what has come out in Aretha Franklin's music, out of the church and into the so-called secular world, carrying all the weight and the force of the religiousness that is there in the beginning. I think it is really interesting to

22. Saliers and Saliers, *Song to Sing*, 5.
23. Saliers, interview, 2016.

think of the music that has come out of Holiness and Pentecostal traditions that then finds its way into genuine secular vitalities and so on, with melodies that carry the old, religious overtones in many ways. It is their performance practice that has changed.[24]

Where entertainment tends to be self-serving, offering the simple, human enjoyment of feeling good and giving access to parts of oneself and one's community, Saliers believes that religious music tends to minimize that kind of self-concern. For him, one way to differentiate between worship and entertainment is to consider the function of each, asking, What does it arouse? What does it sustain? What does it lead to? While both entertainment and worship lead to pleasure, the consequences of each is different:

> The question is in context and intentionality. Does it lead, in fact, to taking delight in the things of God? This includes taking delight in one another, taking delight in people's skills and talents. Does this finally redound to the glory of God? Or does it serve necessarily selfish or egotistical things—though you don't have to place a moral judgment on it. Is it finally something that is carried . . . only for the individual's entertainment, or the preoccupation with the performer's own skills, or the community's own abilities? And since I love so many varieties of music and so much art, I would say that I am profoundly entertained by a lot of it, but what is the line in which my entertainment itself serves transcendence?[25]

Just as it is possible for entertainment to serve transcendence, many people approach a church service as an aesthetic experience. The line between entertainment and worship is not metaphysical or absolute, but rather a matter of context, or a space to explore. Saliers tells a story about Robert Shaw, who would conduct choral concerts in which many people found a sense of transcendence:

> Is that entertainment, or is it something beyond? Is it on the edge of something beyond? Shaw, himself, was kind of jaded about a lot of church stuff. In fact, he used to ask, "Why do they insist on singing such swill, Sunday by Sunday?" That was his approved phrase. Yet when it came to something like the *German Requiem*, he performed it for his wife's funeral. So, there is something that causes a particular piece of music that might simply be for entertainment

24. Saliers, interview, 2016.
25. Saliers, interview, 2016.

and enjoyment to move beyond itself, beyond our own preoccupations, placing us in a much larger context.[26]

Today's debates often end up making the difference between being entertained and worship too clear, pitting contemporary worship in the style of the mega-churches against a more liturgical style featuring classical music and traditional hymns. However, as Saliers points out, the older pattern can often be a disguised form of classical entertainment, in which parishioners enthuse about the way the organist plays Bach or choose a church because of the excellence of the choir. When choirs become overly professionalized, there is the danger of falling into what Saliers calls the commodification of religious experience. On the other hand, sometimes paid musicians become part of the assembly without intending to:

> There were some symphony players hired to do some Taizé music. They thought this was well below them, but they were being paid well for this conference. I watched the symphony bass player, sawing along, yawning, and so on. But about the fifth time through this particular Taizé thing, suddenly I could see that he was paying attention to the singing assembly. Something was going on that was being communicated back to the musician. He got paid, he was a commercial musician, as far as he was concerned this was just religious entertainment. But something got to him in the process of the ritual context of that music and he was caught up as one beginning to worship in some sense. I think there can be cases where we pay for art music, where the music itself as a commercial product actually crosses over the line and begins to serve a community's intention to worship and to glorify the divine.[27]

For Saliers, the line keeps moving between art, entertainment, and worship, describing a borderland where any given event may serve either the ego or God.

Kim Harris: The Unseen Audience

Kim Harris is professor of theological studies at Loyola University's Bellarmine College of Liberal Arts. She is also a musician who writes, records, and produces music as a means to promote creativity, education, social responsibility, and understanding in the world community. Her mass setting,

26. Saliers, interview, 2016.
27. Saliers, interview, 2016.

Welcome Table: A Mass of Spirituals, sets the text of the newly revised *Third Edition of the Roman Missal* to the melodies of spirituals, using recognizable tunes in their totality to present an authentic rendering of the music in the context of the liturgy.

Harris comes at the question of entertainment and worship from the perspective of performance. Wherever she performs she is aware of an unseen audience that exists beyond the people physically in the room. For Harris,

> the unseen audience usually includes the ancestors. It usually includes a larger community of justice, and it usually includes some form of the divine. The universe, or sometimes it is more specific—God or Jesus—something that one would put in that category. I think that is because the spirituals and the freedom songs, because of the intent of the original creating community that we are also trying to bring forward, and because of the history around the songs, usually have that quality of having an unseen audience as a part of it.[28]

Harris's infectious laughter punctuated the conversation as she talked about how the explicit liturgy of a church service affects how people understand the implicit liturgy of a concert. For her, performing at such events is essentially no different from performing in a worship setting.

> There are times when I joke that you can tell the difference between the kinds of performances that we are trying to do by how much writing has to be done. If there is a paper involved, then it is a class, but same songs. If there is an intermission with donuts and coffee, then it is a coffeehouse. Same songs. If the coffee hour comes afterwards, it was probably a church service. Same songs.[29]

Of course, Harris recognizes that there are profound differences between a class, a concert, and a worship service. Nevertheless, she brings not only the same songs, but the same passion and commitment to every venue in which she performs. By telling stories and involving the audience in call-and-response, she invites them into a sacred space where differences dissolve and everyone is invited to encounter the holy:

> That is how my life and my song- and music-making feel to me, as if it is a continuum without a lot of the divisions that are

28. Harris, interview, 2015.
29. Harris, interview, 2015.

sometimes spoken about in terms of what's the difference between a performance and a worship service.[30]

That refusal to differentiate can, in itself, be a mark of God's presence. Sometimes, however, it really is difficult to tell the difference, as Harris points out in her description of the liturgical aspects of a folk music concert. Once, she said, she and songwriter/storyteller Reggie Harris were performing at a music festival in Nova Scotia, where the custom is for people to bring canned goods or a cash donation for the food pantry to the Sunday morning gospel music concert. At this event,

> there might be three, four thousand people. At one point, we said, "This is like church, so here's what we're going to do." I took out a $20 bill and I said, "Here's the $20 challenge: we're going to put it in the plate." [The plate] was somebody's baseball cap. We needed more money, because the food pantry at the shelters really were literally empty. We said, "Now we know some of you already gave." We made it like church. And they raised another five thousand dollars. It was incredible. People knew what to do; in their bones they knew what to do. It was church. It is really interesting how we have these liturgies within us.[31]

Considering the reality that people had already paid a lot of money to attend the event, Harris notes that the food pantry collection worked

> because the unseen audience was there. And they came expecting to be transformed in some way because of the kind of music that it was going to be. That really did feel like performing the gospel for me.[32]

There are also practical differences between different kinds of venues. Harris makes decisions about which song goes where, and about when she will invite the audience to sing along, according to where things fall in the liturgy. She is very specific about using that term, noting that a good folk concert is a liturgy. Nevertheless, an explicit worship service might have more purely instrumental music than a folk concert, especially during a quiet moment when people are thinking about their joys and concerns. Similarly, she does not invite people to sing along during the collection until most of them have their money in the plate, to allow them time to look

30. Harris, interview, 2015.
31. Harris, interview, 2015.
32. Harris, interview, 2015.

for their wallets or write checks. When speaking specifically about worship services, Harris makes it clear that whether she is in a Unitarian church, a Jewish synagogue, or some other religious venue,

> there are conscious and specific times when the unseen audience is invoked. There's going to be some kind of invocation of the divine, there will be a moment for prayers and concerns, where you are thinking about a larger community, and then there's going to be something like a talk or a sermon or a homily where you consciously think about how that is connecting you to a wider community. And because the songs take place in that setting, that does really home them in to the liturgical setting.[33]

In a concert, where there is no explicit invocation or sermon, songs can serve that purpose. For instance, Harris says, in a coffee house

> there is usually not an invocation, but we might sing "Church is Burning Lord" or "Come By Here." There is usually not a time of prayer and concerns, though we might sing the Phil Ochs song, "In the Heat of the Summer." Especially at something like the 50th anniversary of the Watts riots, we might sing that and remember and update the song. And that, in a lot of ways, becomes our sermon for the coffee house.[34]

Harris brings the same passion, the same engaging persona, and the same energetic professionalism to her performances in coffee houses, festival concerts, and worship settings. What changes is her awareness of where she is, who else is present, and the intended purpose of the gathering. And, for Harris, the unseen audience is always part of the mix.

Carl Petter Opsahl: Street Church

Carl Petter Opsahl is a Lutheran pastor, jazz musician, and journalist. In 2002–2003 he was a visiting scholar at Union Theological Seminary in New York City, where he received his doctorate in theology in 2012 with a thesis on spirituality and hip-hop culture, "Dance to My Ministry: Exploring Hip-Hop Spirituality." His other publications include *En fortelling om jazz* (A tale of jazz) and *En god dag. Fortellinger til inspirasjon og ettertanke* (A

---

33. Harris, interview, 2015.
34. Harris, interview, 2015.

good day: Stories of inspiration and reflection) as well as several solo and collaborative albums.

Opsahl would agree with Janet Walton that good worship needs to have an element of entertainment. Called to do outreach ministry on behalf of his denomination, he walks around the city in clerical garb, inviting conversation with anyone who needs someone to listen to them. On Sunday mornings, he puts on liturgical vestments to offer what he calls "street worship," setting up an amplifier, a portable font and altar, communion elements, and candles to create a sacred space in the midst of all the ordinary activities of the neighborhood. When I asked him to describe what happens, he told me:

> The street worship is outside the central train station, so very few of the people there will have seen or noticed announcements. That is such a huge space, so if you don't want to be there, you can just pass by and be somewhere else. When you are in the street, you have not only the commercials on the walls, but you have marketing companies offering tastes of seven different versions of cola. In this very active context, you compete with all these different things, so you have to be more aware of the room, as it were. You definitely should be aware of the room in the church as well, but in the street, you don't know what could happen.[35]

Believing that neither traditional hymnody nor praise music is appropriate in this busy, public place, he has composed service music that draws on his knowledge of New Orleans jazz and Norwegian folk music. For the street worship, Opsahl enlists the skills of an occasional guitarist and an accordion player who is familiar with the music of the Roma people as well as some Asian musical forms, while he himself performs on the clarinet.

Since performance is as integral to street worship as it is to street theater, Opsahl has thought deeply about the difference between good worship and good entertainment:

> It depends on how you define words, for instance. Sometimes you use the word "entertainment." "Oh, it is just entertainment," and that does note that it doesn't really add up to something. Then, sometimes entertainment means that you are feeling good, it is entertaining, your senses are awakened and you are present because you are entertained. And in that last sense, I think worship should be that. And in the first sense, I think when you try too hard to

---

35. Opsahl, interview, 2016.

entertain as a reverend, or doing worship, you will get just at the surface level of engagement. I think for me it has to do with the engagement—if all that is happening engages you.[36]

When asked what it meant to "try too hard," Opsahl made the distinction between authenticity and using tricks in order to get a response, or simply to move from one moment to another. Speaking of his experience as a musician, he says:

> I practice and have some goals. I explore, and sometimes when I play I feel I am really doing new stuff, I am exploring, I am expanding. Or maybe I do something I have done a million times before but still I found just that sound and that phrase, so I feel like I can put all of me in it. The audience might not notice this. Other times, I'm feeling at a dead end and I try little tricks. I know if I play on a high note, OH! Or if I play runs, OH! Sometimes you do these things just to get to the next stepping stone. You are playing and then you don't know where you are going, and you know this will work.[37]

Tricks, of course, is another word for skill. Opsahl is not opposed to using both musical and theatrical skill, along with his sensitivity to the moment, in a formal worship setting as well as in his street ministry. At the opening worship of a recent meeting of the North American Academy of Liturgy, he was asked to begin the service with a clarinet solo. Dramatically playing the first note from the back of the darkened church, he walked through the nave improvising a bluesy tune:

> Playing from back of the church, that is a trick, or that normally that will work. OH, playing back in the church. Wow! Interesting. I thought everything was supposed to happen up there! But that is a trick. Then as you go into that and you see people who are there, and you are aware of the people, and then something happens.[38]

About half way down the nave, Opsahl saw a little boy who put his hands over his ears and looked distressed. As he approached the boy, Opsahl looked directly at him, playing more and more quietly. Gradually, the boy took his hands from his ears and looked back into his eyes. What had begun as a trick became a moment of deep, authentic connection, not only

36. Opsahl, interview, 2016.
37. Opsahl, interview, 2016.
38. Opsahl, interview, 2016.

with the little boy, but with the entire gathered community as they noticed the interaction and smiled at Opsahl, the boy, and one another.

Working in street ministry is another kind of performance. When Opsahl walks out his front door wearing a clerical collar, he is both authentically himself and performing the role of priest. When asked how conscious he is about embodying the church for those who do not normally attend formal worship, Opsahl replied:

> I am very conscious when I put on my collar when I go from home. My ministry starts right there. When I am taking the bus or the subway to my work, I am ready for whatever happens. Sometimes people start conversations on the subway which lead to longer conversations. Sometimes people are in desperate need for something and then I am available for what is happening. I think my training in improvisation has prepared me for that. I am open to whatever is happening. But I have a bag of skills. I do not want to romanticize improvisation. You really need to have skills to improvise.[39]

In addition to his street ministry, Opsahl also offers worship services in a cafe where people gather who struggle with addictions, and in prisons:

> I think it is to address the spiritual needs of people who don't dare to go into church. Or in mosques, for that matter. I meet a lot of Muslims on the streets and in prisons, and when we have announced worships and people to sign up for it, half of the congregation are Muslims.[40]

Opsahl acknowledges that part of the reason imprisoned Muslims show up is that the worship time is an entertainment, or an opportunity to spend an hour out of their cells, but it is also an opening for conversation.

Opsahl believes that entertainment is a good thing in itself. When people come to church, whether it is in front of the train station, in a café, or in a prison, he wants them to enjoy themselves. If that is all that happens, he says, at least they had a good time.

39. Opsahl, interview, 2016.
40. Opsahl, interview, 2016.

Mark Miller: Entertainment as Obligation

Mark Miller serves as associate professor of church music at Drew Theological School and is a lecturer in the practice of sacred music at Yale University. He also is the minister of music at Christ Church in Summit, New Jersey. Since 1999 Miller has led music for United Methodists and others around the country, including directing music for the 2008 General Conference. His choral anthems are best sellers for Abingdon Press and Choristers Guild and his hymns are published in *Worship & Song, Sing! Prayer and Praise, Zion Still Sings, Amazing Abundance, The Faith We Sing,* and other hymnals. When I asked him about the differences and similarities between good worship and good entertainment, he said that he has been trying to define them himself:

> What do those words mean for people? "Entertain" often carries a lighter connotation. "Worship" seems to carry a heavier connotation. Worship seems solemn; entertainment seems light, carefree, something you just pass time, maybe with extra money or something. And worship is more like obligation, maybe something you are supposed to do.[41]

Miller, however, rejects these common distinctions, turning them inside out and questioning the assumptions behind them:

> For me, entertainment should be an obligation, or worship should be considered playful or full of life and whim and all the things that might go to what we consider entertainment. We pay good money for entertainment. We don't expect wonderful worship, and we don't pay money for it.[42]

The result of neither paying for nor expecting wonderful worship is that too often what you get is neither good worship nor good entertainment. On the other hand:

> I go to *Lion King* and have a spiritual experience because it is all about the spirit that lives in us, that draws us together as community. And sometimes I will go to worship and not feel moved at all, and that is probably not good worship. I think that these rituals that gather us together in a time and a place, to take us out of ourselves, to put us in contact with a Higher Power, and put us in touch with the gathered body, the cloud of witnesses, all of

41. Miller, interview 2016.
42. Miller, interview 2016.

those people gathered past and present, in this world to try to pull together community and care for each other—that is true worship for me. If that worship happens authentically in spirit and truth, then I'm going to be drawn into it and feel what I would define as the Spirit of God, or the Spirit moving in that place. Of course, as a worship leader, I'm hoping that that is happening in worship. But I think that it happens in other places, too, that might be considered entertainment.[43]

Like Gordon Lathrop, Miller argues that both worship and entertainment depend on whether those who are leading turn the spotlight on themselves or understand and serve the needs of the community by helping it to go deeper with one another and with God. The danger in both cases is that it might become distorted by egoistic narcissism or misdirected and unfocused:

All the things that we talk about that make good worship—understanding flow and theological content and quality of performance, whether that is leading a prayer, whether that is performing, reading the sacred text, singing a piece of music—all that kind of breaks down the understanding of good worship when it is either ill-prepared or fear creeps in, or if instead of feeling that I am in control all of a sudden I'm stressing out because I don't know what's happening and I'm not leading this right.[44]

While Miller lives and works in the orbit of Broadway, his training and taste lead him to prefer Bach to Sondheim, if only by a small margin. He sees himself primarily as an organist and church composer, but even his most church-oriented music is clearly written with a twenty-first-century sensibility. In addition to his work as a hymn writer and worship leader, Miller composes works that he terms sacred musicals with themes taken from Christian biography or biblical narratives and music that would not be out of place in a Broadway show. Miller uses a different musical voice in these sacred musical theater pieces than he does in hymns designed for congregational singing. However, he says,

I like to blur the two sometimes, so that the musical sacred pieces, like something in a musical, could be sung by a congregation, or certainly by a choir in a sacred music setting. Usually, in a musical setting, I've got a story that is being told, so the music has to

43. Miller, interview 2016.
44. Miller, interview 2016.

connect itself to the inner working of the story. Let's say songs have congregational beats in a worship service, where there might not be that tightly knit flow of telling a narrative. Although it is just occurring to me right now, you could do both. You really should have both in a worship setting.[45]

Indeed, Miller uses secular music in worship as a way to connect with the congregation. While he would not have the congregation sing the theme to a popular TV show, he might sneak it into the incidental music as people are moving after the Doxology or during the offering. He explains that he uses these cultural clues

to make sure people understand that worship doesn't happen out in a universe of its own. It is happening right now, right here. You can't repeat it. It is not, Oh, well, it is time to go to church. No, it is very special. You won't have this moment again. So, let's make it real, and make it understandable. We play a little *Star Wars* clip; I see a teenager who's just seen the movie say, Oh, my God, he's doing that! Trying to connect people to, making connections to what's real all around us. I don't know if I would call it entertainment, but certainly, people need to smile in worship. They need to have "aha" moments.[46]

For Miller, those "aha" moments from the world of entertainment can lead to "aha" moments of awareness of the presence of God:

Hopefully the presence of God is happening in the theater watching *Star Wars*. There is no better theological metaphor that I have found than "May the Force be with you." I have taken it from biblical principles, but it is the best way for me to describe to someone who might not be steeped in theological understanding. What is the Spirit of God? What is the truth of God? Well, let's talk about the Force and what that means. I think it is very serious, delving into great mysteries and understandings of what we believe and how we are as community together.[47]

For Miller, the interplay between entertainment and worship is an important through-line, in which each affects the other, and where God can be found in both. In turning the notions of worship as obligation and

45. Miller, interview 2016.
46. Miller, interview 2016.
47. Miller, interview 2016.

entertainment as play upside down, Miller suggests that good worship and good entertainment are not as different as many might suppose.

Marlita Hill: Dance as Faithful Practice

Marlita Hill is the choreographer and artistic director of Speak Hill Dance Company, based in southern California. She is the author of *Defying Discord: Ending the Divide between Your Faith and "Secular" Art Career* and the book series *Dancers! Assume the Position*, produces a weekly podcast called *The Kingdom Art Life*, and is the creator of "The Kingdom Artist Initiative," a discipleship program for artists working in secular culture. She also serves as the associate director for Edge Project, an organization focused on art, culture, and faith.

Hill considers the question of entertainment and worship from the perspective of a performer and choreographer who frequently is asked to bring her professional skills from the world of dance into the worship environment:

> If you're leading people in worship, it has to present an accurate picture of God and what God has shown in the Word and in relationship with humans. I would say there is a difference between outreach and ministry. There is a difference between outreach and standing before people and leading people into worship. What churches need to define is, Am I creating a place for people to engage with God through this creative environment, or am I trying to lead these people into worship through the arts?[48]

Hill points out that many people believe that anybody should be able to come and worship God with their art in church without any form of judgment about whether it is good or bad as art. She agrees that while this is true for one's personal devotion, God values skilled artists to lead people in the worship context, just as skilled artisans were used to create the tabernacle in the desert and the temple in Jerusalem. Those who wish to dance in worship, she insists, need to invest in becoming more skilled so that God can use them in greater and greater ways:

> Skill is a tricky word: who defines that, and according to what criteria? When I started ministering in dance, I would not have been

48. Hill, interview, 2015.

classified as one with "skill." But I did go to school and invest in the natural ability I had. God used me in every season of proficiency.

The bottom line is people think you should not have to invest in artistic quality, in continuing to develop your skill, if it's for God. The sentiment is, "He takes me as I am and He only looks at my heart." That's true. But that doesn't mean He's okay with you staying there. Each of us should be dedicated to increasing our capacity (and how that is done looks different from person to person). And there are times when He specifically calls the skilled (those who have invested in developing their skill) forward.[49]

Hill thinks that the problem with the concept of performance in church comes from a concern about putting oneself on display instead of pointing to God. When reminded that for some people the concern is more about not being sincere, she rose to the defense of performers:

Only a person who has never been in performance on the other side would say something like that. Not to be confrontational, but unless you've ever performed outside of the church, then you don't know what it is like. You have assumptions of what it is like, but for those of us who have performed as artists in concert work, there is a tremendous amount of sincerity that is required, and a lot of study and dramaturgy. What they are talking about is what we call out here "the Hollywood spirit," which is very presentational: "Look at me, look at me, look at me." But that is the nature of commercial work, because if you have two hundred people in an audition, you have to stand out to get the job. To me, there's nothing wrong with it. It is the nature of the form. It can become problematic when you have a dancer from that strand come into ministry and not understand what it is about ministry that is different. What I mean by that is no, you do not turn off any of the fire that you dance with. It is just getting yourself to understand you are a conduit for the audience to see God. It's simply helping dancers understand they're in a different context, and coaching them in how to thrive in that context without squelching what God has given them, how He's made them, and without shaming the other contexts God has placed them in.[50]

Hill's particular interest, however, is less in dance within the context of a worship service than in helping professional performing artists live for God in their artistic careers. Many artists of faith become frustrated when

49. Hill, interview, 2015.

50. Hill, interview, 2015.

the church discounts their work in the world unless it is explicitly Christian in its content. In her own work as a choreographer, Hill does not particularly seek out Christian dancers or try to put a Christian message into what she presents. Nevertheless, people seem to sense the spiritual aspect of her secular work:

> I enjoy seeing bodies move through space. I'm not trying to say anything, I'm not trying to lead you to think anything, I just believe the body is beautiful in itself. I consistently have people who come up to me and talk about how touched they were and moved they were and they did not understand why. There was just something about it. Now I know what it was. Before I do my choreography, I pray over it. Before my dancers get there, I invite the Spirit of God to be a part of the creative process. . . . Our art life is more than just the art piece. It is also about the process—what are you doing, how you go about creating art, how you go about making business decisions, how do you interact with people. That is important, too. God is involved in all of that.[51]

Hill does not directly engage the question of the relationship between good entertainment and good worship, but rather considers the broader questions of what it means to be a performing artist, both in the church and in the commercial sphere. What is important to her is integrity, skill, and the intention to honor God, whether in a service of Christian worship or in an entertainment venue. Like Tracy Radosevic and Mark Miller, Hill believes that both worship and entertainment, when done well, can lead people into awareness of the divine presence.

Marcia McFee: Performance, Ritual, and Art

Marcia McFee is an author, worship designer and leader, professor, preacher, and artist. Her engaging and interactive style has been called "refreshing," "inspiring," and "unforgettable." McFee combines her background and experience in professional companies of music, theater, and dance with a variety of worship and preaching styles in order to bring a fresh experience of the Gospel to each worship setting. She has provided worship design and leadership at numerous international and regional gatherings.

Along with Radosevic, Miller, and Walton, McFee believes that those who consider performance and entertainment as the antithesis of worship

51. Hill, interview, 2015.

and ritual have not engaged the ideas sufficiently. Noting that this belief gained currency at roughly the same time as the contemporary movement in worship was gaining in popularity, she believes that traditionalists started to use the words "performance" and "entertainment" as a pejorative in reaction to that movement:

> I think what happened is that the word "performance" got connected to theater and concert settings, and anything that smacked of non-traditional began to be seen as performance. And we began to be leery, rightly so, of expressions of worship that were one-sided. Anything that didn't involve the congregation, we began to call performance.[52]

This concern that worship should not be a performance, says McFee, included worries that congregations should not applaud, since that is what audiences do. While some church traditions do give permission for what McFee terms "para-verbals," such as shouting "amen" or other exclamations, as well as clapping, others only include clapping as an acceptable form of response. When performance became suspect, these communities began to stifle such spontaneous reactions:

> So now all of a sudden, we are not clapping, even, and so we have this deadly silence in places where we should have some sort of response. It became this-or-that, very dichotomous. We can't clap, we can't respond because then we are giving glory to the singers, or to whoever has just done something, rather than giving glory to God.[53]

McFee believes that this concern is unfounded. Human beings, she argues, need to offer up a kinesthetic reaction as a part of praise and ritual. Warning that stifling that response cuts people off from reacting to the movement of the Spirit, she sees no harm in clapping when the energy of the moment calls for it. After all, she says,

> God gave the gift to the people and the choir. The choir offers up the gift, and we give thanks to the people for offering up the gift, as well as the content and the praise that it stirred in us. I think we just got ourselves into a bind here. We got very self-conscious

---

52. McFee, interview, 2015.
53. McFee, interview, 2015.

about what clapping means and forgot to pay attention to what the Spirit of the moment actually invites.[54]

Echoing Radosevic, McFee points out that the word "performance" means "to give form," and that not paying attention to performance issues leads to not-fully-formed worship. Like Eileen Guenther, whose thoughts on the subject appear in chapter 5, McFee finds poorly planned worship problematic. When worship is not considered performance, then leaders see no need for rehearsals or walk-throughs. The result, says McFee, is awkwardness and unsureness that detracts from worship.

This concern about performance extends even to those churches where choirs have been replaced by praise bands. While praise-and-worship music is sometimes criticized as being too much like a rock concert, McFee sometimes wishes it were more like one:

> The people on the stage in a rock concert are often more aware of the audience than praise bands are of a congregation. I give this analogy when I'm working with praise band: You know that time in a rock concert when the song that everybody knows is going and the performer, the rock star, takes the microphone and points it at the people and stops singing and everybody else sings the part. The energy in the room just goes through the roof and you feel like you are a body together and you are singing together. And those are some of the favorite moments at a rock concert. But do you ever do that as a praise team? Do you ever make sure that the people get to feel themselves as a body, or are we just drowning everybody with sound the whole time, and you're singing and playing the whole time so that we can't hear ourselves be a body? So, I wish you were more like a rock star sometimes.[55]

For McFee, worship becomes like entertainment in the pejorative sense when the leaders forget that the main goal of ritual is to enliven the congregation in their praise. When leaders ignore this imperative, worship becomes something people just watch rather than fully participate in. Certainly there are many ways to participate, and there will always be times in worship when the congregation watches or listens, but it is necessary to engage the congregation, to choose music that they can sing, and to teach them the songs. This is as true for classical worship accompanied by organs as it is for praise bands.

---

54. McFee, interview, 2015.
55. McFee, interview, 2015.

Ritual, for McFee, is not the repetition of an archaic form, but rather the enlivening of the gathered body, no matter the form or style. She makes it clear that even simple rituals such as bringing in the light of Christ are formative, helping the congregation to connect to the divine. When people come to worship expecting to be affected by what happens, ritual becomes a dynamic interactivity among all who are gathered and between them and God.

Entertainment, on the other hand, is largely done for its own sake, rather than for the sake of this kind of transformation. However, McFee is not willing to draw sharp lines between entertainment, art, and worship. When asked about the Saliers's construct of the church of Saturday night and the church of Sunday morning, she told a story about an earlier time in her life when she was a professional dancer as well as doing dance in the context of Christian worship. Hesitating to call what she did "liturgical dance," which evokes a certain stereotypically meditative and more literal style quite different from what she was doing, she remembers when Carla DeSola saw her work for the first time:

> I had a piece called "In Defense of Creation" when that document came out decades ago, the UMC Bishops' anti-nuclear statement. So I created a piece about it in which the movement was defiant, strong, and more abstract than literal. I worked in the avant-garde dance world in New York City, so I was very comfortable with more abstract movement bringing meaning. So anyway, Carla DeSola is the godmother of liturgical dance, and to be honored as such. She said to me afterward, "Well, that was mighty energetic for a Sunday morning."[56]

Later, at the Greenbelt Festival in the UK, McFee presented a program in which some pieces related to biblical stories and others were expressed in more abstract movement for the sake of whatever the movement evoked:

> A lot was left to the viewer, much like an abstract expression of visual art might. In the Q and A afterwards, somebody mentioned that piece, and said, "What did it mean?" and I said, "Well, what did it mean to you? What did it bring up in you?" And they looked shocked and only said, "uh, uh, ok." In this reaction to art in the midst of ritual we run up against the whole Enlightenment idea that we have to get the one, correct meaning from it. We don't give ourselves permission, or we don't teach people to have permission

56. McFee, interview, 2015.

to think for themselves, and to acknowledge that this kind of thinking would be a spiritual discipline in itself.[57]

McFee had the presence of mind to repeat a small dance phrase from the larger piece, and to ask the audience to say words that it evoked for them. What evolved from the responses was the feeling of transformation—of turning a problematic moment into something joyful. Indeed, she calls the moment sacred, saying that if a dance or another artwork evokes reflection in people, then it is fit for worship.

Exploring the Territory

Most of the people whose views are recounted in this chapter seem to believe that the difference between good worship and good entertainment may be found less in what is done than in what intentions and expectations the participants bring to the experience. Several specifically mentioned the difference between a congregation and an audience, stressing that a congregation comes for the purpose of actively worshipping God together, while an audience comes to be passively receptive of whatever the performers are presenting. Others considered the question from the point of leadership, noting that those who lead worship have a particular responsibility to service, while entertainers do not. Most agreed that both good worship and good entertainment require a certain level of preparation, attention to detail, and practice, as well as the ability to adjust in response to whatever is happening in the moment.

The source of the remaining areas of disagreement lies deep in the past, not only of the specific speakers, but also in the collective history in which entertainment and worship have been intertwined. To help us understand how the past has shaped these issues, the next chapter will explore some of the paths that both worship, entertainment, and the performing arts have travelled, from their indistinct and shadowy beginnings to the intersecting and often confusing roads that they are following today.

---

57. McFee, interview, 2015.

three

The Only Show in Town

From the twelfth century on, the chief action they could glimpse through the rood-screen that separated nave from chancel was the elevation when the priest raised the consecrated host above his head. Seeing this moment came to be the high point of the mass and people were known to shout "Heave it higher sir priest" if they could not see and adore.[1]

FROM THE EARLY CHURCH'S insistence that actors must renounce their trade or be refused burial in Christian cemeteries, through the theatrical understanding of the Mass in the Middle Ages and its disavowal in the Puritan rejection of many celebratory customs, to the contemporary accusations that one or another worship style is "mere entertainment," Western culture has exhibited a long-running love/hate relationship with the performing arts.

For most of human history, worship and entertainment were often indistinguishable. When someone told a story around the campfire, the deities and spirits were as palpably present as the hunter's skill, the antelope's speed, or the cunning of the lion. Every tree or clearing had its local spirit. The clear distinction between sacred and secular that seems so integral in the post-Enlightenment West was not as obvious in the past or even in some cultures today, where storytelling and the dramatic traditions that grow from it are often still indistinguishable from religious practice.

1. White, *Brief History*, 88.

A brief review of how religious faith was performed in previous eras may shed some light on various current worship practices and their relationship to entertainment. As this history approaches the modern era, the road will turn toward England and then North America, which is the primary geography of this study.

Drama and Ritual in Hebrew Scripture

As theater historian Dale Savidge recounts, very little has been written about Israelite drama and ritual. While there is no archeological evidence nor any indication in the Hebrew scriptures that the ancient Israelites built theaters,

> one need not have a theatre building to have theatre. Evidence of dramatic structure can be found in at least three biblical books, and there are further examples of theatrical performances among the prophets.[2]

These theatrical performances are a natural outgrowth of any oral tradition in which family stories are told and retold through the generations, becoming over time the founding stories of a people. It is hard to believe that these stories were not at least partially acted out, embellished with exaggerated facial expressions, gestures, and maybe even accents to denote people from different places. It is fairly well established that the Hebrew scriptures began in this way. Eventually, these stories were written down and codified, becoming what is now known as the Bible.

Once it was written down, however, the Bible continued to be transmitted to most people orally. After all, very few people could afford to own a manuscript of any kind. Indeed, in most places, the only copy of a biblical text would belong to the community as a whole, usually in the custody of the priests, making reading scripture aloud necessarily a communal and theatrical affair. It is difficult to separate the religious from the social (or entertainment) aspects of such communal readings.

The book of Nehemiah recounts one such communal reading. The book as a whole relates what happened when some of the exiles who had been living in Babylon returned to Jerusalem in the sixth century BCE. In Nehemiah 8, the people are celebrating the rebuilding of the city's defensive wall. All the people—men, women, and children old enough to

2. Johnson and Savidge, *Performing*, 25.

understand—have come together in an important civic space, where a *migdal* (literally a tower, and variously translated in this context as a stage or platform) has been erected so that the person addressing the crowd might be more clearly seen and heard. The passage describes the considerable stagecraft that marks the singular importance of the occasion, as the priestly scribe Ezra stood on the platform flanked by representatives of each of the twelve tribes. The reading lasted from early morning until noon, as

> Ezra opened the book in the sight of all the people, for he was standing above all the people; and when he opened it, all the people stood up. Then Ezra blessed the Lord, the great God, and all the people answered, "Amen, Amen," lifting up their hands. Then they bowed their heads and worshiped the Lord with their faces to the ground.[3]

As the people fell on their faces overcome with emotion, the political ruler Nehemiah, along with Ezra and the Levites, admonished them, saying that this was not a day of mourning, but one of celebration. As the passage notes:

> Then he said to them, "Go your way, eat the fat and drink sweet wine and send portions of them to those for whom nothing is prepared, for this day is holy to our Lord; and do not be grieved, for the joy of the Lord is your strength." So the Levites stilled all the people, saying, "Be quiet, for this day is holy; do not be grieved." And all the people went their way to eat and drink and to send portions and to make great rejoicing, because they had understood the words that were declared to them.[4]

While it is unknown how much those farthest away from the stage were able to hear in that time long before electric amplification, the story emphasizes the widespread participation not only in listening to the reading, but in the communal drama of building booths to live in, "each on the roofs of their houses, and in their courts and in the courts of the house of God, and in the square at the Water Gate and in the square at the Gate of Ephraim."[5] Hearing a long-forgotten scripture read aloud in this dramatic setting, surrounded by a huge crowd, was almost guaranteed to arouse strong emotions, and the priests and Levites were well prepared to help

3. Neh 8:5–6.

4. Neh 8:10–12.

5. Neh 8:16.

manage the crowd as they gathered branches as they had been instructed in the reading.

While the occasion related in Nehemiah 8 is particular to the return of the exiles to Jerusalem from captivity in Babylon, it may reflect more general reading customs in the context of religious gatherings of the period in which participants are both audience and actors. Savidge distinguishes formal dramatics, which are prepared by actors for presentation to an audience and generally involve rehearsals and prepared scripts, from informal, creative, or educational dramatics. It is unknown how much of the event in Nehemiah 8 was scripted and rehearsed, and other semi-theatrical events in scripture reflect a more informal approach. Savidge suggests as examples such events as David's attempt to appear insane in 1 Samuel 21 or other instances in which someone pretends to be ill or to be someone other than they actually are. In particular, he cites 2 Kings 13, in which Elisha tells the king to enact a message from God:

> With great detail the author records how Elisha directs the king to shoot an arrow, even going so far as to place his hands on the king's hands. He then instructs the king to strike the arrows on the ground, and after the king does so three times, the message is delivered.[6]

Similarly, Jeremiah 13, 19, 24, and 27 recount God's instructions to the prophet to do various actions that dramatize the divine intention. And while it may be argued that none of this was done as theater in the sense that is meant today, Savidge suggests more formal dramatics may have been presented in the tabernacle or the temple:

> Recent studies have theorized that the stories collected in the Bible, recorded for us as historical narratives, may originally have been performed in Hebrew worship. This argument is supported by the fact the culture of the ancient Israelites, at least until the time of Joshua, was built on an oral tradition. . . . Such performances may have employed storytelling, with a single speaker maintaining his own personality while relaying the story through voice and gesture. Or they may have involved an ensemble of actors imitating the characters of the stories in a performance encased in the worship rituals.[7]

6. Johnson and Savidge, *Performing,* 26.

7. Johnson and Savidge, *Performing,* 27.

Savidge is building a case for the legitimacy of drama in contemporary Christian life, relying on educated guesses rather than documentable facts. While his picture of dramatic presentations of historical narrative in the context of worship in ancient times is intriguing, it is only speculation. On the other hand, it is probably fair to assume that in ordinary life, people did tell stories to entertain one another as well as to instruct the children. It is also reasonable to assume that, as in any time or place, some of those who told stories had a more dramatic flair than others, taking on the roles of heroes, villains, and even angels and demons, regardless of whether this was in a formal religious setting or around the domestic hearth fire on an ordinary evening. While the origin of drama may lie in such informal storytelling, there is incontrovertible evidence for the connection between religion and theater in ancient Greece and Rome.

Religious Drama in Greece and Rome

Because Christianity came into being in the Greco-Roman world, it is common to trace the development of both drama and religious practice in the West through pre-Christian Greece and Rome. Much has been written about the origins of ancient Greek theater in the public recitation of the *dithyramb*, a type of choral song to the god Dionysus, as early as the sixth century BCE. Early records seem to indicate that processions or parades and sacrifices to the gods were held in the theater, as well as competitions between tragedians. This conflation of worship of the deities and popular entertainment was so important to Greek civic life that virtually every city built an open-air amphitheater and funded the annual dramatic competitions so that the entire populace could gather to laugh and cry together.[8]

In Rome, the situation was more complex. While huge arenas were built to entertain the people with gladiatorial contests, chariot races, and mimes, no permanent theaters were allowed within the city prior to what is now known as the Theater of Pompey, built in conjunction with a temple to Venus Victrix and dedicated in 52 BCE. Prior to that date, temporary wooden structures had been built to accommodate theatrical performances, which, as in Greece, were closely tied to religious festivals. While most of the plays themselves were not specifically about the particular deity or

---

8. It is not clear whether it was considered proper for married women to attend these performances, although enslaved women and the prostitutes known as *hetaerae* seem to have been present.

events the festival was intended to commemorate, their placement within the context of religious observances as well as the proximity of performance sites to temples indicates a close relationship between theater and religious observance. In his essay "Religion in Roman Comedy," Boris Dunsch notes:

> The religious character of the games becomes obvious also in the practice of *instauratio*, the restarting of a play in cases when it had been interrupted somehow or when even the smallest omission or disturbance had occurred during its performance. In such a case a play, like any ritual, had to be reperformed from scratch.[9]

Furthermore, and perhaps more to the point, virtually all such plays incorporated scenes in which religious rituals were portrayed. As Dunsch points out, the boundary between ritual and entertainment is fluid, depending on context and intended function, as well as who carries it out, where it takes place, and under what circumstances:

> If the aim of the performance is to effect transformations, then the performance is a ritual. If the aim is entertainment, then it is theatrical drama, although perhaps no performance is ever purely ritual or exclusively entertainment. In principle, all drama can also (and is often expected to) effect transformations, and every ritual can be effective in entertaining.[10]

Thus, in the early Christian era, when sacred acts like baptism were portrayed on stage for the purpose of ridiculing Christian beliefs, there was a danger that parts of the theatrical action could turn into real and binding sacraments. So closely were drama and religious rites intertwined in the Roman world that the *Apostolic Tradition*, composed around 215 and generally attributed to Hippolytus, advised actors (along with prostitutes and their pimps, painters and sculptors of idols, participants in gladiatorial contests, and heathen priests, among others) to find some other form of employment if they wanted to become Christians.[11] Indeed, Christian opposition to the theater as well as all other pagan entertainments continued to be so strong that the emperor Justinian closed all public theaters in 625 CE, in response to their objections.

9. Dunsch, "Religion," 635.
10. Dunsch, "Religion," 635.
11. Hippolytus, *Apostolic Tradition*. Part II §16:9–16.

Dramatic Liturgy After Constantine

While theater, as such, was never a part of the early church, much has been written about the dramatic nature of worship, especially after Christianity became a state religion under Constantine. In *Do This: Liturgy as Performance,* Richard D. McCall writes:

> There is a seemingly irresistible temptation to speak about the liturgy of the Christian Church as somehow "dramatic." Theodore of Mopsuestia was not the first, but he was certainly the most systematic of the fourth-century theologians to describe the actions and the participants in the Holy Eucharist as representative of something other than what they appeared, in their liturgical functionality, to be. He tells the catechumens that in the offertory procession they must see Christ being led to his passion and in the deacons who enact "the invisible ministering powers when they carry up the offering."[12]

McCall goes on to cite Dionysius the Pseudo-Areopagite, Maximus Confessor, Pseudo-Germanus, Amalarius of Metz, and other ancient authorities as the source of the allegorical and dramatic understandings of liturgy popularized in the Middle Ages and continuing well into the twentieth century.

In his description of the fourth century homilies quoted in the discussion of symbols in chapter 4, Edwin Yarnold calls the early baptismal rites "spine-chilling." While they may not seem that way today, that is because it is difficult for modern people, who are used to electric lights and instant communication, to imagine how it must have felt to be a candidate for Christian baptism, being led through utter darkness to ceremonies about which they had been told nothing in advance. Yarnold notes that the Greek word for such a person is *catechumen*, which means "person under instruction" or "hearer," adding that the equivalent word in Latin is *audiens* or *auditor*, from which comes our word "audience."[13] However, the catechumens were not merely an audience for the baptismal rites. They were the primary participants.

Baptisms were most often held in the middle of the night, frequently during the Easter vigil. Several weeks earlier, those seeking to become

---

12. McCall, *Do This*, 2, citing Theodor of Mopsuestia, Homily 15, chapter 26.

13. Yarnold, *Awe-Inspiring Rites*, 7.

Christians were subject to one or more exorcism rituals. Of these, Yarnold writes:

> Two elements were involved in the ceremony of exorcism: a form of words by which the devil was bid to go out from the person: and the gesture of blowing. This act of breathing signifies that the devil is, so to speak, blown away. It was a conventional gesture to express contempt: for example, to breathe on the emperor's statue constituted a treason.[14]

After these preliminaries, the catechumens fasted, prayed, and went to the church either early in the morning or in the evening after their daily work was finished to learn about Christian beliefs and history. Therefore, by the time of the Easter Vigil, they were probably both chronically hungry and sleep-deprived. At some point between midnight and dawn on Easter morning, accompanied by singing and prayers, the catechumens were led out of the assembly and taken to the baptistry, which was often a building separate from that in which other services were held, then stripped naked and either plunged under water or made to kneel in a large pool while water was poured over them, often with little or no explanation. After this:

> the naked neophyte was dressed, not in the clothes he wore before, but in white. These white robes were a symbol of the life of the resurrection to which the new Christian had now passed, and of the innocence that should now distinguish him.[15]

Dressed in white, the new Christians, now called "neophytes," were led back into the main church building and allowed to participate in the Eucharist for the first time. These exits and entrances were dramatic not only for the neophytes, but also for the worshippers who were gathered on what was arguably the holiest night of the Christian year as they waited for the proclamation, "Christ is risen." As they watched the catechumens leave in their ordinary clothing and return as baptized Christians, hair still wet and skin glistening with oil from the various anointings, the connection between baptism and dying and rising with Christ was underscored.

In addition to the famous homilies presented by Yarnold, which were intended to explain the mysteries of baptism and Eucharist to the newly

---

14. Yarnold, *Awe-Inspiring Rites*, 28. Notes 19 and 20 in this paragraph refer the reader to Cyril of Jerusalem, *Procat. 9*; John the Deacon; St Augustine, *Op. Imperf. ConAgra Jul.* iii.199; and *Patrologia Latina* 45.1333.

15. Yarnold, *Awe-Inspiring Rites*, 28.

baptized, there is at least one other witness to the dramatic nature of worship in the earliest Christian centuries. Perhaps the earliest attestation to the conflation of entertainment and worship is a manuscript written in the early fifth century by a woman who is most commonly known today as Egeria. Her writings are variously referred to as *S. Silvia Aquitaine peregrinate ad local sancta, Peregrinatio Aetheria,* and *Itinerarium Egeriae.* The manuscript gives no indication about the circumstances of the author. Taking the form of letters to her sisters, it is not even clear if these sisters are biological relations or members of a religious order, or in what country they may have resided.[16]

Scholars trying to put a firm date to Egeria's account of her travels note that she quotes verbatim from Jerome's Latin translation of Eusebius' *Onomasticon,* published after 390 CE, and mentions other texts which she probably could not have seen earlier than 403 or 404. Other authorities place the date around 417, noting that her description of the celebration of the Feast of Ascension corresponds to historical evidence regarding the dedication of the Basilica of the Nativity in that year, while others suggest a somewhat later date, closer to the middle of the century.

The extant twenty-two pages seem to start in the middle and several pages seem to be missing. A number of documents by other writers in later years suggest familiarity with some version of the text, and supply some clues, but little can be known for certain about the beginning or the ending of Egeria's journey, or how long it actually lasted. Indeed, she gives very little specific information about what any given place looks like, instead paraphrasing scripture or other works she considered authoritative.[17]

What her account does give is a reflection of the dramatic quality of the liturgy in fifth-century Jerusalem, in which different churches or areas were reserved for specific commemorations and celebrations. In his comments on the work, translator George Gingras reminds us:

> It is not to her that we should turn for specifics on the prayers recited, the Psalms and hymns sung, or the precise rubrics followed. Frequently she tells us that the hymns and prayers were appropriate to the day and the place, but only rarely does she even tell us what scriptural passages were read at the various services. However, for anyone seeking an overall view of the liturgy celebrated

16. See Gingras, "Introduction," in Egeria, *Egeria,* 2–7.

17. Gingras, "Introduction," in Egeria, *Egeria,* 20.

in Jerusalem, and especially for a panorama of the great feasts, her descriptions are unique.

A picture of the general religious life of Jerusalem, particularly the degree of participation of the people in the rituals, may also be gleaned from these pages. If nocturnes and the daily morning office were essentially monastic services, a multitude, including many children, attended daily vespers. On Sundays, the crowds were as large as at Easter. On the great feasts, particularly Palm Sunday, Holy Thursday evening, and Pentecost, vast throngs moved from the Mount of Olives to the city. Egeria states that on Pentecost not a single Christian remained at home.[18]

It is important to note the theatrical nature of these events, in which the pilgrims as well as the local Christians were kept moving from place to place in order to both edify and entertain them. Many of them, after all, had nothing else to do since the pilgrims, at least, were in Jerusalem for no reason other than to be present at the physical places described in scripture. For instance, on the day before Palm Sunday, there was an elaborate recre-ation of Jesus' entry into Jerusalem. Gingras writes:

> Egeria is the first author to describe the dramatic imitation of Christ's entry into Jerusalem that was to become one of the church of Jerusalem's most significant contributions to the liturgy. The emphasis was clearly on *imitatio,* for the bishop re-enacted the role of Christ, being led "in the same manner as the Lord once was led" (*in eo typo quo tunc Dominus deductus est*). The elaborate ritual began at the seventh hour (early afternoon) when "all the people" assembled at the Eleona on the Mount of Olives. At the ninth hour they moved to the Imbomon, the site of the Ascension, where at the eleventh hour there was a reading from St. Matthew's account of Palm Sunday. A procession then formed and slowly descended the mountain with the people chanting the refrain, *Blessed is He who comes in the name of the Lord,* and with the children bearing olive branches and palm fronds. The procession moved through the entire city and terminated at the Anastasis, where vespers was celebrated.[19]

Egeria recounts dramatic representations and readings of the Sermon on the Mount, the betrayal by Judas, Jesus' appearance before Pilate, and many other events of Holy Week. She describes various processions at

18. Gingras, "Introduction," in Egeria, *Egeria*, 26.
19. Gingras, "Introduction," in Egeria, *Egeria*, 35–36.

midnight or dawn, during which participants sang psalms and other songs; a three-hour service before the cross on Good Friday; the baptism of the catechumens during the Easter vigil; and many other events.[20] Even at this early date, there is a blurring between worship and play-acting, between ritual and entertainment, in these attempts to dramatize the scriptural events. It is not that individuals took on roles in order to act out the narrative, but rather the entire congregation was imaginatively constituted as the crowds following Jesus around Jerusalem, Bethlehem, and other places during the events of Holy Week.

In Egeria's account of the church-sponsored events in fifth-century Jerusalem, there is a lot of ritual taking up a lot of time, and most of it is not the Mass as it is understood today. Rather, it is a way of keeping the pilgrims engaged. The pilgrims clearly came to Jerusalem out of a sense of piety, of wanting to walk where Jesus walked. Far from encouraging a disembodied spirituality, these rituals were meant to engage all of their senses. For instance, Egeria writes of a procession which begins in Bethlehem, ending in Jerusalem at dawn on the feast of Epiphany. Later, she says, everyone gathers

> in the major church on Golgotha at the beginning of the second hour. It would be superfluous to describe how the churches—the Anastasis, the Cross, and the church in Bethlehem—are decorated on that day. You see nothing there but gold and gems and silk. If you look at the hangings, they are made of silk with gold stripes; if you look at the curtains they are also made of silk with gold stripes. Every kind of sacred vessel brought out on that day is of gold inlaid with precious stones. How could the number and weight of the candle holders, the candelabra, the lamps, and the various sacred vessels be in any way estimated and noted down? And what can I say about the decoration of this building which Constantine, with his mother on hand, had embellished with as much gold, mosaics, and marble as the resources of his empire permitted—and not only the major church, but the Anastasis as well, and the Cross and the other holy places in Jerusalem?[21]

The sumptuousness of the decorations must have been overwhelming, especially since everyone was somewhat sleep-deprived after the all-night vigil and the long, slow, six-mile walk up the mountain from Bethlehem to Jerusalem. Similarly, the dramatic Holy Week observances are filled with

20. Gingras, "Introduction," in Egeria, *Egeria*, 38.

21. Egeria, *Egeria*, 95 (chapter 25).

"hymns and antiphons appropriate to the day and place . . . and there are likewise readings from the scriptures."[22] Egeria repeats this formula of "appropriate to the day and place" frequently in her writings, pointing out that wherever she goes, there are constant reminders of what happened in that place at that time of year. On the morning of Good Friday,

> a throne is set up for the bishop on Golgotha behind the Cross, which now stands there. The bishop sits on his throne, a table covered with a linen cloth is set before him, and the deacons stand around the table. The gilded silver casket containing the sacred wood of the cross is brought in and opened. Both the wood of the cross and the inscription are taken out and placed on the table. . . . The bishop, remaining seated, grips the ends of the sacred wood with his hands, while the deacons, who are standing about, keep watch over it. There is a reason why it is guarded in this manner. It is the practice here for all the people to come forth one by one, the faithful as well as the catechumens, to bow down before the table, kiss the holy wood, and then move on. It is said that someone (I do not know when) took a bite and stole a piece of the holy cross. Therefore, it is now guarded by the deacons standing around, lest there be anyone who would dare come and do that again.[23]

After all have touched the wood with their forehead, looked at it and finally kissed it, a deacon presents the ring of Solomon and a vial with which kings were anointed, so that the faithful may kiss the vial and venerate the ring. To conclude what must have been an incredibly moving and perhaps somewhat frightening experience, all the people crowd together in the "large and beautiful courtyard" between the cross and the church known as the Anastasis, listening to the bishop read psalms and other scripture passages about the passion "from the sixth to the ninth hour." Egeria comments:

> At each reading and at every prayer, it is astonishing how much emotion and groaning there is from all the people. There is no one, young or old, who on this day does not sob more than can be imagined for the whole three hours, because the Lord suffered all this for us.[24]

22. Egeria, *Egeria*, 104 (chapter 31).

23. Egeria, *Egeria*, 110–11 (chapter 37).

24. Egeria, *Egeria*, 112 (chapter 37).

While neither the baptisms described by Yarnold nor the pilgrimage rites described by Egeria are, strictly speaking, theater, they may most certainly be understood as participatory drama. As such, they may be seen as occupying the borderland in which worship and entertainment are nearly indistinguishable from one another.

Medieval Europe

In the popular imagination, the church is often envisioned as the only source of entertainment and diversion from the hard sameness of life in medieval towns and villages. Many historians have insisted that there were no dramatic productions of any kind after the fall of Rome, and whatever need or desire for drama or amusement had to be filled, so the story goes, by going to church. There is a certain truth to that idea: even the simplest Mass was inherently dramatic, with the priest and altar-servers wearing vestments unlike anything that ordinary people wore, reading from ornate books in a language that most people did not understand, swinging thurifers that spread fragrant smoke throughout the sanctuary, ringing bells and saying words that turned bread and wine into the body and blood of Christ lifted high for all to see.

Perhaps more to the point, in the late Middle Ages, at least, most people went to Mass regularly, with those who were particularly devout (or had more free time) sometimes attending more than one service every day. However, to envision their attendance as somehow similar to today's custom—everyone arriving at approximately the same time and participating together in responsive readings and prayers, listening to the sermon, and singing hymns—is to misrepresent Christian worship in that period. Rather, since every priest was required to say Mass daily, most churches, at least those in the larger parishes or in close proximity to monasteries where there were many priests, had multiple Masses going on more or less simultaneously throughout the day. While the priests were reciting their prayers, the ordinary people were absorbed in their own devotions, such as reciting the rosary, praying the Stations of the Cross, or immersed in the prayers and images in the small prayer books referred to in England as "primers." In addition, as church historian James White notes,

> There was plenty to see in the nave itself from the painting of
> the last judgment over the chancel arch, to saints painted on the
> walls and glazed in the windows, to sculptured images in wood

and stone everywhere, to the images of the deceased on the floor beneath their feet. The whole building was a textbook of saints of the past and warnings of the future.[25]

Seeing the consecrated Host at the moment when the priest elevated it over his head was particularly important. In this period, receiving the bread and wine of communion was relatively rare, with most people only doing so at Easter. Instead, people believed that simply seeing the newly consecrated Body of Christ was enough to connect them with the divine, that the practice that came to be known as "ocular communion" was perhaps even more efficacious than actually eating the bread and drinking from the chalice. Since the Latin Mass was often not only incomprehensible but also inaudible to most of the people present, a bell was rung just before the priest said the words of institution, "*hoc est enim corpus meum*" (this is my body). This "sacring bell" allowed everyone in the church to stop whatever else they were doing and walk over to the appropriate altar. As Eamon Duffy relates:

> [The] arrangement of Masses allowed the laity to see the Host at several sacrings within a short space of time. The warning bell might summon devotees at prayer in another part of the church, or even hearing a sermon, to view the Host. At Exeter the bishop legislated to prevent sacring bells being rung while the choir Offices were being recited, in case the clergy and choir should be deflected from the task in hand. The early fifteenth-century Lollard priest William Thorpe was enraged when preaching to a crowd of lay people in the church of St Chad in Shrewsbury, "bisiinge me to teche the heestis of God," when "oon knyllide a sacringe belle, and herfor myche peple turned awei fersli, and with greet noyse runnen frowardis me"[26] to see the Host at an altar elsewhere in the church.[27]

Apparently, the frequent devotional activities of the faithful were less widespread in countries other than England, since, as Duffy points out,

---

25. White, *Brief History*, 90.

26. "Beseeching me to teach the commandments of God," when "someone knelled a sacring bell [to announce the elevation at another altar], and therefore many people turned away fiercely, and with great noise ran away from me." [Translation by author with assistance from James Estes]

27. Duffy, *Stripping*, 98.

an Italian visitor to fifteenth-century England, commenting on the notable devotion of the laity, wrote that "any who can read tak[e] the Office of our Lady with them, and with some companion recit[e] it in the church verse by verse in a low voice after the manner of the religious."[28]

While Duffy insists that these were the practices of the devout, there seems to have been at least some aspect of entertainment involved, as witnessed by the following vignette that he relates from a letter that the fifteenth century landowner Margaret Paston sent to her husband, who was away on business:

> The glimpse Margaret Paston affords us of the devotional habits of her neighbour, Sir John Hevingham, who went to church one morning and heard three Masses, "and came home again never the merrier, and said to his wife that he would go say a little devotion in his garden and then he would dine," could in its essentials be matched for hundreds of the well-to-do in the period.[29]

Paston does not suggest that Sir John was anything other than devout, but there is something in his merriment on coming home from hearing three Masses that suggests he went there as much for amusement and pleasure as for genuine worship. While "merry" in this period did not have the connotation of levity that it has today, there is a sense that this is something that the leisured classes did to pass the time, to see and be seen. For Sir John and people like him, both going to Mass and saying devotions in the garden seem to have been a kind of pastime, a divertissement, as Geoffrey Moore whose interview appears in chapter 6, might put it, albeit a diversion that might actually lead to an encounter with God. On the other hand, several of the other people whose voices are heard in this volume might wonder why worship shouldn't make one merry, either in the older sense of the word or today's usage.

Listening to sermons was also a popular pastime in the Middle Ages. Sermons were not generally offered as part of Mass. Rather, preachers set up in other parts of the church building, or even outdoors on the church porch that opened onto the village square, frequently gathering a large crowd. It was not always clear that people came for edification rather than for entertainment. As Anne Hudson points out in her study of a manuscript containing sermons dated to around 1410:

28. Duffy, *Stripping*, 212.
29. Duffy, *Stripping*, 99.

Because on the whole sermons are supposed to be edifying and only incidentally diverting, they have never been everyone's favourite form of entertainment. Yet, if the mediaeval preachers attempted to alleviate the tedium with *curiosa* (under which general heading were included stories, titbits of arcane lore, rhymes, jokes, and an elaborate confection of divisions and subdivisions), there was a widely recognized danger that audiences would come to expect such trifling fare and would protest or walk out if they were offered sound, but unadorned instruction in lieu.[30]

As one particularly aggrieved preacher wrote,

These days mochyl folk wyl nowt lowyn hem to syttyn doun at the sermoun, ne welyn heryn it with meek herte, but thei welyn stondun that they moun redely gon awey yif the prechour plese hem nout. Summe comyn obstinat in here synne. . . . Summe comyn only to heryn coyouste and newe thyngis. . . . Summe comyn only to be seyn. Some comyn only for the maner and for non devocion ne for no profyght of here soule and swyche fallyn sone on slepe.[31]

It seems clear from records such as these that the church, if not the only show in town, was certainly one important place where people went to be entertained as well as edified, and that they felt free to leave if the preacher was boring. More intentional entertainment may have been more difficult to find. Positing a theatrical void beginning with the closing of the theaters in the sixth century, many theater historians have traced a development that begins with a few lines from the tenth century Benedictine liturgy for Easter morning. In a small piece of musical embellishment that came to be known as the *quem quaeritis* tropes, the liturgy relates the story of the women who come to anoint the body of Jesus. In a brief dialogue, the angel asks them *"Quem quaeritis in sepulchro, Christicholae?"* In response, the women reply, *"Jesum Nazarenum crucifixum, o caelicolae."*[32] Some rubrics suggest that this was sung responsively by cantor and choir while the

---

30. Hudson, "Sermons," 223.

31. Hudson, "Sermons," 223. "These days many folk will not allow themselves to sit down at the sermon, nor will they hear it with a meek heart, but they will stand so that they might readily go away if the preacher does not please them. Some come obstinate in their sin. Some come only to hear curiosities and new things. Some come only to be seen. Some come only according to the custom and not for devotion nor for their soul's well-being, and such have fallen sound asleep." [Translation by author with guidance from James Estes.]

32. Cargill, *Drama and Liturgy*, 20. "Who are you looking for in the sepulcher, Christ-followers? The crucified Jesus of Nazareth, o heavenly ones." [Translation by author]

priest and his retinue were walking toward the altar, heightening the drama of the moment.

From this simple beginning, increasingly complex dramatic renderings of biblical narratives here held within the walls of the church. In his *Christian Rite and Christian Drama in the Middle Ages*, O. B. Hardison affirms the popular notion of the church as the only show in town but dates dramatic reenactments in worship to at least a century earlier than the earliest known manuscripts that contain the *quem quaeritis*:

> Religious ritual *was* the drama of the early Middle Ages and had been ever since the decline of the classical theater. The most valuable source for our knowledge of ninth century attitudes is the *Liber officialis* of Amalarius of Metz, who died around 850 but whose influence can be discerned in liturgical commentaries throughout the later Middle Ages. The *Liber officialis* shows, first, that the Mass was consciously interpreted as drama during the ninth century, and second, that representational ceremonies were common in the Roman liturgy long before the earliest manuscripts of the *Quem quaeritis* play.[33]

However, despite the assertions that there was no theater at all in Europe after the sixth century, many popular entertainments never quite disappeared, and they too contributed to the development of theater in Europe. While in the medieval period the church was probably the primary source of diversion from the everyday difficulties of life, other forms of entertainment were available, at least some of the time. These included minstrels and troubadours who entertained the wealthy, as well as traveling theatrical troupes, puppeteers, acrobats, and even hucksters who used mime, rough comedy, and spectacle as a way to drum up business on market days in towns and villages.

By the twelfth century, some dramatizations of scriptural stories had moved out of the church and into the streets as the civic celebrations that came to be known as the mystery play cycles. Miracle plays, which recounted the stories of various saints, seem to be related as well. Over time, these plays became increasingly secular, in England eventually culminating with the great age of Elizabethan drama in the sixteenth century.

To the assumption that the early attempts at drama were simply amateur efforts by the local monks, Oscar Cargill suggests that they may have employed some of those wandering minstrels to write and produce plays

---

33. Hardison, *Christian Rite*, viii.

that would attract pilgrims to visit a tomb or behold the relics of some hero.[34] Or, perhaps they "employed the minstrels . . . to keep the local communicants at home, to provide them with instruction and entertainment."[35] Regardless of the reason, Cargill notes,

> it is possible to show that, while amateurism may be assumed in a great deal of the work, the better plays are probably the product of trained artists, of men who had previously made a living by their mimetic abilities in minstrelsy.[36]

As Hardison points out, examination of two twelfth-century manuscripts, the *Mystère d'Adam* (Mystery of Adam) and *Sainte resurrección* (Holy Resurrecton), shows

> that there existed a vernacular tradition in the twelfth century, and that this tradition was already independent of the Latin drama from which it is usually said to be derived. Although the history of this tradition is unknown and probably unknowable, its characteristics can be determined from the plays themselves. The evidence indicates that they are consciously composed works, written for a theater that already possessed definite traditions of staging and acting, and conceived from the beginning as representation.[37]

Perhaps the drama of the liturgy was the only show in town prior to the emergence of the great dramatic cycles that moved out of the church into the streets of York, Chester, Wakefield, and other places in England around the thirteenth century—or perhaps there was an independent theatrical tradition that existed outside the church for a number of centuries prior. Either way, it is clear that dramas dealing with mystery, miracle, and morality were an important form of entertainment in towns and villages in England throughout this period. While the record differs in detail in the rest of Europe, the general outlines remain the same.

Renaissance, Reformation, and Counter-Reformation

Along with the rise of a new, humanist approach in both theology and the arts, theatrical entertainments moved farther and farther away from the

34. Cargill, *Drama and Liturgy*, 132.
35. Cargill, *Drama and Liturgy*, 134.
36. Cargill, *Drama and Liturgy*, 131.
37. Hardison, *Christian Rite*, ix.

church in the Renaissance. The commedia dell'arte, which began in Italy and spread throughout Europe in various forms, increased the repertoire of stock characters that had been familiar from the earlier morality plays, and expanded the subjects that plays could address. In sixteenth-century England, Shakespeare and his contemporaries offered plays that depicted the inner lives of the characters, from kings to ordinary people. Elsewhere in Europe, humanist writers looked back to the classical drama of Greece and Rome as examples for their own theatrical experiments. Even the theater took on a new look with the invention of stage sets behind a proscenium arch facing rows of spectators in a building designed for the purpose, rather than the movable stage wagons that went from place to place, as was characteristic of the civic mystery play productions.

Meanwhile, Christian worship was also changing, especially in those areas most affected by the Protestant Reformation. The inherently multisensory Roman Catholic Latin Mass, with its sumptuous vestments and dramatic ritual, was replaced in Protestant areas by a style of worship characterized by long sermons, didactic prayers, and Bible readings, all in the vernacular. In many Protestant congregations, congregational hymn singing took on a new importance, as did the often-unaccompanied singing of metrical psalms.

In response to the reformers' accusations about the abuse of indulgences and the problems of a largely uneducated and often venal clergy, the Catholic Church instituted its own reforms, which became known as the Counter-Reformation. Music took on an even greater role with the development of the pipe organ, which served both to accompany choral singing and as a source of purely instrumental music in cathedrals and the larger churches. James White writes:

> For those Roman Catholic parishes and religious communities with an abundance of talent, the mass became an imposing concert of performance music. Ever since the ninth century, an alternative to the chant had been developing in the form of polyphonic music with different words and melodies sung simultaneously. By the end of the twelfth century, composers were writing for three or four voices and polyphony had become a distinct alternative to plainsong.[38]

In addition, the Council of Trent mandated sermons on all Sundays and holy days as part of the Mass:

38. White, *Brief History*, 136–37.

Archpriests, curates, and all those who in any manner soever hold any parochial, or other, churches, which have the cure of souls, shall, at least on the Lord's days, and solemn feasts, either personally, or if they be lawfully hindered, by others who are competent, feed the people committed to them, with wholesome words, according to their own capacity, and that of their people; by teaching them the things which it is necessary for all to knew unto salvation, and by announcing to them with briefness and plainness of discourse, the vices which they must avoid, and the virtues which they must follow after, that they may escape everlasting punishment, and obtain the glory of heaven.[39]

One result was that Catholics as well as Protestants, for whom preaching became central to any worship service, built new churches that were for listening as well as for looking. As White notes, "The Jesuits, particularly, distinguished themselves in preaching campaigns. Their churches were designed specifically with the acoustical needs of preaching in mind and the pulpit became an important liturgical center."[40] He continues:

The paradigmatic building was the main Jesuit church in Rome, II Gesu, built 1550–1572. Not only did the choir disappear as a distinct space, not only was preaching accommodated by careful consideration of acoustics, but the whole space became a theatrical setting for the mass. In these new churches, roodscreens disappear, and the chancel is more a stage, as in the theater.[41]

Indeed, says White, the look of Il Gesu and many other churches built by the Jesuits was influenced by stage design.

For Protestants, in contrast, new buildings were less ornate so as not to detract attention from the sermon. The pulpit became central, and balconies brought the congregation closer to the preacher so that they would not miss what was being said.[42] This emphasis on the spoken word and on scripture, rather than on the spectacle of the Mass, is connected with the deep suspicion not only of theater and theatricality, but of entertainment generally that characterized much of Protestant morality during the Reformation. In many smaller towns and villages, particularly, as in previous

---

39. Council of Trent, Session V, Second Decree, § 2.

40. White, *Brief History*, 134–35.

41. White, *Brief History*, 139.

42. White, *Brief History*, 139.

eras, there was not much organized entertainment other than whatever was going on in church most of the time.

The Puritans, in particular, attained a reputation for being serious and prudish, particularly after they banned many popular traditional pastimes like Maying, bear-baiting, and Morris dancing. Under their influence, in 1642 Parliament expressly closed all the theaters in London. However, it is not entirely clear that the Puritans deserved their anti-entertainment reputation, since they did engage in sports, literature, music, and other artistic pursuits, as long as they did not interfere with work or prayer. As a recent article on the website of the Congregational Archives in Boston notes:

> Although Puritans objected to the use of music in church as distracting and "Popish," they frequently enjoyed singing and playing instruments in the home. Similarly, dancing was all about context; many denounced "promiscuous dancing" (i.e., both sexes dancing together) as they felt it could lead to fornication, but folk dancing that avoided physical contact between men and women was generally permitted.[43]

Other Protestant groups drew the lines in different places, with some discouraging any kind of frivolity, especially on Sundays, and others permitting a greater freedom of expression in all of the arts while still emphasizing the primacy of work and prayer.

Today

The critique of the conflation of worship and entertainment today is widespread. Some of it is deserved, as in this recent article in the *Washington Post* about a congregation that is giving away cars to entice people to come to church. As *Post* staffer Julie Zauzmer vividly writes:

> If the pastor had ever wanted to channel his inner Oprah, this was his chance.
>
> "You ready to give a car away?" Stephen Chandler boomed into his microphone, bouncing in his boots at the altar Sunday. And then the pastor did it again. And later that day, he would do it again. And again. Five free cars in all, handed out to the lucky winners at Destiny Church in Columbia, Md., on Sunday. "We were just going for something you would not expect a church to

---

43. Congregational Library, "Puritans and Entertainment."

do," Chandler said. "This is something you would not expect a church to do."

It was part marketing ploy—but also theology, Chandler said. Randomly giving away cars to people who show up to worship demonstrates God's unbelievable, no-strings-attached goodness, Chandler preached. And it sure helps get people in the door on a Sunday morning.[44]

While a church adopting the values and techniques of a game show give-away or a carnival raffle seems like a particularly crass example, many other houses of worship are borrowing ideas—and sometimes the same performers and artists—from the world of entertainment in order to get people in the door. At the same time, certain entertainment venues are taking on some of the trappings of worship.

Altar Call in the Concert Hall

Entertainment is usually what people expect when they go to a rap concert. In a comment from the audience after a presentation at the 2018 Biennial Conference of the Association for Practical Theology, someone referred to concerts at which Chance the Rapper invited his audience into worship. Startled, I attempted to transcribe what the speaker said. My notes read:

> Corporate worship in the concert space. Chance gave an altar call at a recent concert, saying "Does anyone want to go to heaven?" Fantazia is reinventing a creedal affirmation. Snoop just released a gospel album. There is a long history of Black artists sacralizing whatever space they are in.[45]

At these words, there was a lot of head-nodding and murmured agreement in the room, so clearly this is a phenomenon that is widely familiar to those who were present. As a White woman in her seventies who rarely goes to concerts of any kind and almost never listens to hip-hop or rap, it was difficult for me to follow much of this conversation. What was clear is that those who attend such concerts do not find any contradiction in entertainers inviting them into something like a worship experience, explicitly and intentionally blurring the line between worship and entertainment.

---

44. Zauzmer, "New Spin."

45. Personal notes dated April 14, 2018.

Later in the conference, Karen E. Mosby presented a paper called "'I Speak to God in Public': The Black Millennial Theology and Artivism [sic] of Chance the Rapper." Mosby noted that she takes Chance the Rapper as an exemplar of, rather than an exception to, his generation of Black young adults in the US. In her paper, Mosby argues that Chance's linking of Christian faith, artistic expressions, social activism, and philanthropy as an African-American young man living in the twenty-first century in the United States is not simply his personal viewpoint but is actually shaping a particular brand of what she terms "millennial resistance" to injustice, especially in the African-American community. "Leveraging hip-hop music, fame, and finances," she writes, "he contextualizes God within the realities of Black young adult lives."[46]

While her paper does not mention the so-called altar call which piqued my interest in Chance the Rapper, Mosby does write about the intentional interweaving of the singer's faith with his music. Discussing the lyrics in his 2016 album *Coloring Book*, Mosby notes that they

> transgress the boundaries between hip-hop music and Gospel music; secular and sacred; "conscious" rap and holy rap music. It is art and activism; nostalgic and prophetic; theological discourse and a chronicle of youth fun. It provides a counter narrative to the narrative of the bounded spaces of many churches where young adults are required to check their personhood in the vestibule before entering the sanctuary. These types of congregations provide no room or little room for young adult realities that do not come packaged or articulated in familiar Christian tropes. Chance problematizes these models of Protestant evangelical Christianity that often segregate God-talk from talk about real life.[47]

Mosby's interest is more in the ways that Chance the Rapper navigates the confluence of art, faith, and social action than in any explicit connection between worship and entertainment. However, she also observes,

> the success and critical acclaim of *Coloring Book* accelerated a demand for more of Chance's voice and presence as well as his artistic genius. People wanted to know the how's and why's of what he had produced. They wanted to understand how a hip-hop album could feel like a Sunday worship service, but maintain the rhythms

46. Mosby, "Speak to God," 2.
47. Mosby, "Speak to God," 5.

of a Friday or Saturday night club. How did he manage to tap into Gospel and be true to hip-hop music with integrity?[48]

Perhaps Chance the Rapper's ability to make a hip-hop album feel like Sunday Worship is similar to Kim Harris seeing no difference between her performances in a church or a folk festival, or Don Saliers's reminder that the performance style of earlier generations of Black musicians came out of the music of the Pentacostal church. Recalling that Mosby takes Chance the Rapper as an exemplar of his generation rather than an outlier, his easy conflation of hip-hop and Gospel, faith and popular culture, further blurs any easy distinction between art, entertainment, and worship for at least some of those who attend and put on concerts, as well as those who organize and participate in Christian worship.

Blurred Lines at the Basilica

At the time of this writing, several other events that exemplify the trend to conflate worship and entertainment came to my attention within the span of a few days. The first was a Facebook post about a light show entitled Aura, held nightly except Sundays at the Notre Dame Basilica in Montreal. The basilica is an active Roman Catholic church, with daily Masses and an active parish life.[49] The Aura presentation is held at 6 p.m. and 8 p.m. in the Notre-Dame-du-Sacré-Coeur chapel, which is used during daytime hours as a place of contemplation, prayer, and meditation in the presence of the Blessed Sacrament. While the website of the basilica has a prominent link to the Aura website, no explanation is offered as to the connection between the two or how Aura came to be presented in the basilica.

Aura does not pretend to be a service of Christian worship. It was created by the Moment Factory, an international multimedia design company whose mission statement declares:

> At Moment Factory, we bring people together. Our shows and destinations pioneer forms of entertainment that offer the world new experiences. Whether at a concert, a flagship store or across an urban square, we aim to inspire a sense of collective wonder and connection.[50]

48. Mosby, "Speak to God," 7.
49. Basilique Notre-Dame de Montreal, "Masses and Adoration."
50. Moment Factory, "About."

The Aura website is very clear that there is no religious content, stating, "The spectacle's mission is to encourage spectators to discover or rediscover the beauty and richness of the Basilica's many patrimonial and culturally significant works."[51] However, the websites's description of the "luminous experience in the heart of the Basilica" uses language that suggests, though never quite promises, a spiritual, if not expressly worshipful, experience. The opening splash screen declares:

> Light unveils the richness of the Notre-Dame Basilica's heritage and invites us to celebrate its beauty.
>
> The experience begins with a path of lights, revealing the Basilica's wealth of exquisite works. A progressive immersion into a sonically and visually captivating universe guides visitors to the heart of Notre-Dame.
>
> Then, light, orchestral music and grandiose architecture combine to create a unique, three-act multimedia spectacle.
>
> Allow yourself to be transported by Aura and discover an unexpected, stunning universe presented upon one of the most sublime canvases imaginable: the Notre-Dame Basilica.[52]

While the websites of both the Basilica and Aura are careful to keep the religious mission of the Basilica separate from the entertaining, non-religious spectacle, its placement in the midst of the oldest neo-Gothic church in Canada, with a history that extends to the founding of Montreal in the seventeenth century, suggests that attendees will at the very least make a connection between this immersive experience and the more conventional religious events that take place in one of the most important spaces in the building. That many do make this connection is very clear in the nearly four thousand public comments to a Facebook video describing the sound-and-light show,[53] as readers bring their understandings and preferences about Christianity's relationship to entertainment to the conversation. A small sampling indicates the range of comments:

> Amber Machelle Huls: What are you doing this weekend? Oh, just popping some ecstasy and going to church. Praise Jeebus!
>
> Andrea Hoadley: That's what I was thinking. its beautiful but is it Godly?? These places are the reason why us Christians have

51. Moment Factory, "FAQ."

52. Moment Factory, "Work/Aura."

53. Comments to "Montreal's Basilica Hosts Light Shows." Posts reproduced retain the original punctuation and spelling.

had to defend church period. Is this what the money is for? The money that people are supposed to drop in a jar . . for what? To be the most popular or prettiest? All ego sake.[sic]

Elena Mae Hadley: Andrea Hoadley so thousands of years of ornate cathedrals are misplaced in your opinion? there are plenty of simpler houses of worship if that is what you support but for a long time the church has gained followers and demonstrated power through the construction, elegance and detail of the architecture and art

Another thread begins:

Sammi Glass: I find it interesting that some people are so angry that this church paid an artist to make a beautiful art display of light, but I doubt a single one of those angry has ever given a second thought to the art on the Sistine Chapel, or the construction of St. Peters Basilica and how much money those took. . . . Just saying, grand displays of artistry and beauty in the name of the church and God is not new.

Janet Walters: Sammi Glass times have changed and paintings done hundreds of years ago and are of a religious quality are one thing but a light show is to gaudy for a church. It belongs at a Rock concert.

Someone else argues,

Sadie Cupit: The reason people are mad is because instead of using their money to help people, they used it to create an attraction to get more money from people.

In general, the online conversation exemplifies several widespread attitudes about the relationship between Christian institutions, the arts, and entertainment. Many of the writers castigated the church for spending money on art when it could have been spent on the poor, or for using what they judged a tasteless spectacle as an evangelical tool. Others expressed appreciation for the beauty and wonder of the show, making connections between it and the great church-sponsored art of earlier centuries. Finally, the implicit assumption held by many that the church paid the artists was refuted by those who pointed out that the cost of tickets probably more than covered the expense of the installation, and that it was entirely probable that at least some of the proceeds went to the church for other purposes.

Whether the church paid for the spectacle or saw it as a money-making venture, however, is in some ways a side issue. The primary problem for most of those who chose to comment, as in the car giveaway, was in the blurring of the lines between legitimate outreach and tawdry commercialism—between attracting people through the arts in an authentic and faithful way, and cynically using the tools of commercial entertainment to draw them in, as a churchy bait and switch.

A Beyoncé Mass

The attitudes expressed in the online comments about the light show in the basilica show up in one way or another in almost every conversation about worship and entertainment. They were certainly not absent in discussion of the "Beyoncé Mass" held on April 25, 2018, under the auspices of The Vine SF at Grace Cathedral in San Francisco. Known for its support of music and the arts as well as the diversity of its largely progressive congregation, Grace Cathedral is the third largest Episcopal cathedral in the US. As the cathedral's Wednesday evening contemporary service, The Vine SF was launched in March 2017, hoping to attract "urbanites and spiritual seekers" with "great music, progressive theology and new connections."[54]

Beyoncé, of course, is a towering figure in the popular entertainment world. Frequently using religious imagery in her songs and videos, she is sometimes referred to as a goddess in the minds of her millions of devotees. In an essay entitled "About the Beyoncé Mass," the dean of the cathedral, the Very Reverend Dr. Malcolm Clemens Young, acknowledges the controversy that surrounded the event, noting "criticisms from our fundamentalist brothers and sisters that Grace Cathedral worships Beyoncé rather than our Lord Jesus."

> For our April 25 Vine worship service, the Rev. Yolanda Norton, Assistant Professor of Old Testament at San Francisco Theological Seminary, will be preaching. Rev. Norton created a "Beyoncé and the Hebrew Bible" class at the Seminary that draws on Beyoncé's music to raise awareness about the spiritual experience of Black women and the issues they face in our society.[55]

While it is not usual, it is also not unheard of to call a service of Word and Table a "mass" at an Episcopal church. A photograph of the special worship folder shows a relatively unremarkable order of worship, with

54. Grace Cathedral, "Vine."
55. Young, "About the Beyoncé Mass."

scripture readings, prayers, sermon, and communion punctuated by songs from the Beyoncé playlist in places that might otherwise be occupied by congregational hymns and choir anthems. Perhaps the most controversial piece, other than the songs themselves, was the Lord's Prayer, which was introduced with the instruction, "Said by all, with the language below, or the language of your heart." The bulletin then included the traditional text beginning with "Our Father, who art in heaven" alongside a Womanist Lord's Prayer beginning with "Our Mother, who is in heaven and within us."[56]

In an online video report called "Finding God at a Beyoncé Mass," Rev. Jude Harmon, who co-presided with Norton at the Mass, responds to a reporter's question about progressive theology, saying, "Honestly, I think that Beyoncé is a better theologian than many of the pastors and priests in our church today." A little later in the video, Norton explained how the lyrics of Beyoncé's "Flaws and All," which was sung during communion, can be construed as prayer:

> She has this ambiguous audience right in the song. Maybe it's Jay-Z, maybe it's her fans. I love it when she says, "I'm a train wreck in the morning, I'm a bitch in the afternoon. Every now and then without warning I can be really mean to you." What we do in the worship service is we make that about a conversation that we would have with God. So if you imagine that as a prayer to God, "I don't know why you love me / And that's why I love you"—Right. "I neglect you when I'm working"—Yep, we all do that. So it is really about naming Black female spirituality as embodied in that song.[57]

While some would accuse the organizers of this worship service of going too far by elevating a pop entertainer to near sainthood in its attempt to attract the young and hip, others defend their actions, noting the overflow crowds in this outreach to Black women as well as LGBTQ persons and others who have been marginalized by the church and society.

Whether one is a fan of Beyoncé or not, this event does raise the ongoing question of whose music is allowed in church. Similar concerns were expressed in the 1960s, when jazz greats Vince Guaraldi and Duke Ellington both composed what were termed "concerts of sacred music." When Guaraldi's setting for Eucharist was performed at Grace Cathedral,

56. MTO Staff, "Episcopal Church."
57. "Finding God," video.

his trio accompanied a sixty-eight member choir. One report alluded to a less-than-favorable reception of such secular music in worship, noting:

> Some attendees were uneasy about it and complained to the Rev. Charles Gompertz that it sounded like supper music, to which he replied, "Of course. What does Communion represent but the Last Supper?"[58]

While the somewhat glib response may seem like a cheap shot, the pastor was reminding his listeners that music for worship does not have to be solemn or ancient in order to help worshipers connect with God. Similarly, Duke Ellington's forays into church music got mixed reviews. As jazz historian David Brent Johnson notes, while Ellington's own sacred concert at Grace Cathedral had a better reception than Guaraldi's, a planned performance in Washington, DC, at Constitution Hall in 1966 was not as welcome. Instead, there was

> intense opposition to it from the city's Baptist Ministers Conference, which represented 150 area churches. Reverend John D. Bussey declared that Ellington lived in ways opposite from what the church stood for, denounced his performing in nightclubs, and called his music "worldly."[59]

Not coincidentally, the Vatican banned jazz masses in 1967, calling them "distortions of the liturgy" and "music of a totally profane and worldly character."[60] This is not unlike the problematic reception of the gospel music that is so widely accepted as part of the African-American church experience today as it moved out of radio and the concert hall and into the church. As Cleophus LaRue notes:

> Gospel music and gospel choirs, for example, framed the style of many Black Baptist churches in the first half of the twentieth century. So offensive was gospel music to some in mainline American Black Protestantism that some churches were known to throw out the gospel singers. Michael Harris, in *The Rise of Gospel Blues*, reports that one of the gospel singers who got thrown out of church in the early part of the twentieth century was a woman named Mahalia Jackson. Shortly after moving to Chicago from New Orleans, Jackson joined a group named the Johnson Singers, which

58. Johnson, "Sacred Blue."
59. Johnson, "Sacred Blue."
60. Johnson, "Sacred Blue."

sang gospel music throughout the city. But when a Chicago pastor heard this new type of music called *gospel* music, he was so offended that he threw Jackson and her group out of his sanctuary, saying, "Get that twisting and jazz out of this church." On her way out the door, Jackson looked back at the pastor, no doubt in a tone of defiance, and said, "This is the way we sing down south."[61]

Like the accusations of impropriety regarding the use of Beyoncé's music in church, jazz in the 1960s and gospel earlier in the twentieth century were denounced as popular entertainment rather than legitimate art forms performed by highly trained artists. This raises the question of whether the preference for Mass settings by Bach or even Leonard Bernstein in a service of Christian worship might be a matter of class and taste rather than one of sacred versus secular intent. Indeed, one might ask similar questions over the controversies that arise when churches abandon venerable hymnody in favor of praise choruses that share characteristics of melody and rhythm with certain kinds of popular music. Once again, the question becomes framed in terms of whether what is being performed can be classified as art or entertainment. If art is good for the church but entertainment is bad, who decides what is art and what is entertainment?

Wedding as Spectacle

Not long after the Beyoncé Mass, the entire world was invited to witness the wedding of England's Prince Harry and the American actress Meghan Markle, broadcast live on television and streaming to electronic devices everywhere. In a *Washington Post* article the next morning, the writers explicitly call it a "professional, well-produced, secure, one-performance-only global entertainment . . . meant to propagate the royal brand and introduce viewers to the next act in the long-running drama known as the House of Windsor."[62] While this characterization of the event is somewhat tongue-in-cheek, it also recognizes that not just royal weddings, but weddings in general, are very often considered more as a form of entertainment or spectacle than as serious rituals with very real consequences for the people involved. Brides and grooms, as well as parents, other family members, and friends, spend considerable time, effort, and money on organizing the set,

61. LaRue, *Believe I'll Testify*, 41.
62. Booth and Adam, "Prince Harry and Meghan Markle's."

the decorations, the costumes, and the food. Wedding planners are often so intent on getting the best photographs and videos that pastors or other officiants find themselves ignored when they object to any arrangements, repeatedly discovering that for many the show takes precedence over any religious or communal meaning.

In the case of the royal wedding, this mixing of spectacle and ritual was heightened by the fact that the groom's grandmother is the titular head of the Church of England. Whatever the young couple's private beliefs and tastes, the liturgy and language of the church gave a certain gravitas to the proceedings, reminding both the congregation within the church walls and the vast audience tuning in from wherever they were that this was, first and foremost, a service of Christian worship. The pageantry in this case was not due to someone's whim, but rather was appropriate, as Egeria might have said, to the time and place. Although the congregation was filled with figures from the world of entertainment, they were not present to entertain but rather to witness one of their own community take on a very different kind of lifetime role, as a member of the royal family. As in the medieval era, the sober yet magnificent celebration of the rites of the church became, in many ways, the only show worth watching for millions of people all over the world.

On With the Show

Whether or not the church was ever the only show in town, it is clear that today there is plenty of competition. The assumption that worship is, or should be, inherently dramatic began well before the Christian era and continues into discussions about worshipful entertainment and entertaining worship today. Likewise, the idea that there is something inherently suspect in the theater, or even in all the arts, is already evident in some of the earliest Christian witness and continues to be seen in the ongoing accusations that some kinds of worship are too much like entertainment. At the same time, many forms of entertainment use elements of ritual and tradition in a way that invites the audience into a spiritual or even worshipful experience.

In the interviews presented in this volume, as well as in more casual conversations in churches, classrooms, and around seminary lunch tables, the subject of worship and entertainment frequently elicits passionate opinions. These discussions reveal that a large portion of the disagreements hinges on how speakers and listeners define not just worship and entertainment, but other related words that are equally open to multiple interpretations. The next chapter examines some of these words and the ways that they reveal different assumptions about their meanings and about what is valued both within the church and more broadly in the wider society.

four

Matters of Definition

"When I use a word," Humpty Dumpty said, in rather a scornful tone, "it means just what I choose it to mean—neither more nor less." "The question is," said Alice, "whether you can make words mean so many different things." "The question is," said Humpty Dumpty, "which is to be master—that's all."[1]

THE OPINIONS HELD BY those whom I interviewed seem to fairly represent a similar range that might be heard if any group of North American Christians were asked to talk about worship, entertainment, and the arts. Whether they still attend the kind of church that their parents took them to when they were children, or have sampled many different styles of worship, the vast majority seem to have some opinion about the relationship between worship and entertainment, as well as what kind of worship they prefer. As we have seen, those opinions range from seeing worship and entertainment as opposing poles to entertainment as an essential component of worship. These differing viewpoints are real and cannot be ignored.

People want worship to be deep, meaningful, and authentic. They want to feel that they belong there, that they have a part, and that they know what is going on. They want to know that God is present, and that God

---

1. Carroll, *Through the Looking Glass*, 123.

loves and forgives them. What differs is how they have come to experience these fundamental elements of Christian life.

Sometimes, though, much of the argument comes down to a matter of definitions. Often, people use words loosely, and a listener/reader for whom certain words have very specific and tight definitions may disagree not due to a dispute with the underlying intention of the speaker or writer, but because the other person has used a word or phrase for which the listener/reader has a very particular, and very different, definition. It is not that one or another definition is literally definitive or more correct, but rather that definitions arise out of experience, which may include various areas of professional specialization, as well as geographic, social, or denominational location. This chapter examines the varying definitions of some of the most important words in the discussion, so that they can better serve as guideposts in exploring the terrain.

Art

While entertainment is so often considered problematic, especially with respect to worship services, the arts have had a long, distinguished career in the Roman Catholic tradition and have been making a comeback in many Protestant circles in the past thirty or forty years. Music, of course, has been an important art form in most Christian traditions, with congregational hymns and choral singing of one kind or another a staple of orders of worship for most of the history of the church. Poetry, particularly in the form of prayers, canticles, and hymn texts, has usually been acceptable, although not always recognized as an art. Dance and drama, on the other hand, have been in and out of favor in different periods, and the visual arts have been alternately celebrated as windows into heaven and vilified as idolatry.

In the modern period, art has become for many a source of revelation. Both in the secular world and in the church, artists are often revered as prophets and seers who make visible the invisible and speak truth to power. Meanwhile, as noted above, entertainment is often viewed with disdain both inside and outside the church. Those who provide light hearted material, in particular, are often dismissed as mere entertainers, in distinction from serious artists, who are thought to produce music or dance or theater or even film from the depths of their souls.

This distinction between entertainment and the arts is a relatively recent one, growing out of Renaissance ideas about individual genius and

Enlightenment notions of aesthetics and disinterested contemplation. In his recent volume *Art Rethought,* philosopher Nicholas Wolterstorff traces the history of these ideas. Presenting what he calls the "grand narrative" of art and cultural history, he notes that

> what was new in the early modern period in Western Europe was thus not that the arts first put in their appearance; the arts had always been there. Also not new was that the works of the arts were engaged as objects of contemplation; that had always been one of the ways in which they were engaged. What was new was the increasing prominence, among the newly rising middle class, of contemplation as a way of engaging works of the arts in secular civil society.[2]

This new emphasis on contemplation, and its associated practices of collecting and connoisseurship, led to new ways of evaluating and ranking the arts. Before the eighteenth century, most writing about the arts was directed to the artists themselves, focusing on skills and attitudes for practicing music, poetry, architecture, painting, and so on. This approach can be seen as early as Aristotle's *Poetics,* in which, as Wolterstorff points out, "[A]fter making some preliminary comments about the nature of drama, Aristotle offered guidelines for the construction of a good drama."[3] Over time, attention in writing about the arts shifted from practical advice for the artist to the public practice of disinterested contemplation. Wolterstorff quotes art historian Paul Oskar Kristeller's 1965 essay "The Modern System of the Arts" extensively in his discussion of the rise of the eighteenth-century notion of the fine arts as a reflection of the social and cultural conditions at that time. Wolterstorff writes:

> The most important of those conditions was . . . "the rise of an amateur public to which art collections and exhibitions, concerts as well as opera and theatre performances were addressed. . . . The fact that the affinity between the various fine arts is more plausible to the amateur, who feels a comparable kind of enjoyment, than to the artist himself, who is concerned with the peculiar aims and techniques of his art, is obvious. . . ." Medieval writers typically associated painting not with music but with such activities as embroidery and goldsmithing; they associated music (by which they sometimes meant music theory) with mathematics. This makes sense if one's focus is on making; producing a painting is

2. Wolterstorff, *Art Rethought,* 7.
3. Wolterstorff, *Art Rethought,* 8.

a good deal more like goldsmithing than like composing music. But if one's focus is on contemplation, then it becomes plausible to group painting and music together, along with sculpture, poetry, and architecture.[4]

The specific fields included in lists of "the arts" have varied, sometimes including such things as landscaping or omitting sculpture. In *Why Art Cannot Be Taught*, art historian and critic James Elkins writes:

The system of the arts has gone through a number of variations. In the late Middle Ages, the Renaissance, and the early Baroque period, what are now called the "fine arts" were mixed in with what are now called crafts, mechanical arts, and sciences.[5]

Elkins cites Charles Perrault, whose 1690 treatise *Le Cabinet des beaux arts* included eloquence, poetry, music, architecture, painting, sculpture, optics, and mechanics in his list of the arts, as one example of such attempts at classification:

It wasn't until the middle of the eighteenth century that the fine arts were at last separated from crafts and sciences. One important early formulation separated arts that are strictly for pleasure from those that have a use (and the author added a third category for arts that were both pleasurable and useful) . . . [while] the eighteenth century codified that idea that there are exactly five fine arts: Painting, Sculpture, Architecture, Music, Poetry.[6]

Other arts, like opera, dance, and gardening were sometimes added by others. More recently, various new kinds of arts have proliferated, such as performance, video, computing, neon, and holography, while activities like ceramics and weaving have returned from their previous exile as crafts. However, what has remained stable since the Enlightenment is the unifying notion that the appropriate way of engaging such works is through aesthetic contemplation or, to use Wolterstorff's clarification in contemporary language, absorbed attention.[7] This way of engaging the arts is largely an elitist project. Citing an essay on persons of "a polite Imagination [sic]" by Joseph Addison published in *The Spectator* in 1712, Wolterstorff notes,

4. Wolterstorff, *Art Rethought*, 10, citing Paul Oskar Kristeller, "The Modern System of the Arts," in Kristeller, *Renaissance Thought II*.

5. Elkins, *Why Art*, 49.

6. Elkins, *Why Art*, 50.

7. Wolterstorff, *Art Rethought*, 12.

"The eighteenth-century writers on the arts were unapologetically elitist in their attitudes,"[8] adding the explanation that, for Addison, "polite" meant "cultured."

> The idea of a cultured person had been employed by the European aristocracy for some time. The idea was now being taken up as a social ideal by members of the middle class of Addison's day; they wanted to become cultured. Addison is addressing these people and arguing that to become cultured they must acquire "taste" in the arts, that is, the ability to recognize and revel in beauty. . . . Addison bases his case for this being what a polite person will do in his or her leisure time on the claim that, in thus engaging the arts, one experiences "the pleasures of the imagination," these being pleasures of a kind to be preferred to all others.[9]

By contrast, Wolterstorff notes, intellectual pleasures were deemed to be exhausting and perhaps dangerous to one's health, while sensory pleasures were considered "gross, unrefined, and morally dubious; they make a wise man blush. They are the pleasures of the vulgar, that is, of ordinary people, not of the wise and the polite."[10] Of course, Addison and his contemporaries neglect to notice that the arts, like the morally dubious pleasures that they deride, also depend upon the senses. This is implicit in the very word "aesthetic," which at its root is less about beauty than about things that are perceptible to the senses. After all, what is an anesthetic but something that causes one to lose the ability to feel anything at all?

These distinctions may seem familiar to anyone who has engaged in what is often termed the culture wars in the local church. For instance, the organist wants to play only classical music because it is uplifting, while the people in the pews prefer praise choruses or country tunes. Or, the arts committee wants to bring in works by difficult contemporary artists, and the people in the pews would rather have something that looks like the Precious Moments Chapel. These discussions often extend into the secular realm, as the same people who champion classical music and difficult contemporary artists in church might occasionally admit to seeing an arthouse film or documentary while implicitly criticizing those who go to the movies just for fun. While these differences may seem trivial on the surface,

8. Wolterstorff, *Art Rethought*, 14.

9. Wolterstorff, *Art Rethought*, 15.

10. Wolterstorff, *Art Rethought*, 16.

they are, as Frank Burch Brown points out in *Good Taste, Bad Taste, and Christian Taste*, the source of persistent conflict.

Christian attitudes about the arts are complicated by a theological attitude that elevates the spiritual over the sensory. Brown writes:

> Whatever the practice of churches with respect to the arts, many theologians have said that the arts of sense, imagination, and material making are for the spiritually immature, the beginners. In their estimate, spiritual adults will prefer, rather, to contemplate intellectual or spiritual beauty, which is infinitely higher. With some notable exceptions, one finds variations on this theme reiterated from Augustine (354–430) and Pope Gregory the Great (c. 540–604) up to the present time.[11]

Even those theologians who reflect positively on the love of beauty often move very quickly to a definition of beauty that has little to do with the senses, but rather extols the perfectly sublime, spiritual beauty of God. Many people find it almost embarrassing to be seriously worried about matters of taste and aesthetics, and such differences often fall along denominational, class, regional, or racial and ethnic lines. Brown argues that matters of taste and style are not marginal to spirituality, but rather are a serious religious and theological issue. Indicating the depth of emotion that such matters reveal, he writes that

> among the most bonding of joys is the discovery that one's tastes are mutually shared. By the same token, among the most alienating of disappointments is the discovery that a beloved person or admired group rejects the very kinds of art and beauty that one cherishes or through which one worships. These are sensitive matters. If you attack my devotion to Arvo Pärt's contemporary musical style of spiritual minimalism, I may well feel that you don't understand something important about the inner meaning of my faith. If I criticize your unbridled enthusiasm for singing praise and worship choruses from texts projected onto a screen, that may strain our capacity to belong to the same local church. It may even strain the notion that we belong to the same church in a larger sense.[12]

Indeed, such differences about the arts not only divide local congregations, but often also make it less possible for people from different cultural

11. Brown, *Good Taste*, 4.
12. Brown, *Good Taste*, 30.

contexts to worship together. When some people dismiss, as irrelevant to genuine spiritual growth, artworks or music that others cherish and make central to their spiritual and devotional lives, they lose sight of the importance of the arts in opening people to the presence of God in their midst. Of course, it is always possible to disagree in good faith about whether a particular instance of using the arts in worship is a legitimate way for the congregation to offer its prayer and praise to God, or is a "mere entertainment," offered more for the ego gratification of the performers than for the building up of the Body of Christ.

Drama

"Drama" is sometimes used as a synonym for something exciting, emotional, or intense. The word is derived from an ancient Greek word that meant "to do" or "to work." However, it has come to be used primarily with respect to theater, movies, or television, where it generally means a story in which actors depict characters who are in some sort of conflict or tension or danger. Drama is usually thought of as serious, in contrast with comedy, which is typically more light-hearted and intended to elicit laughter.

"Drama" is also used to suggest situations in which people take strong positions against one another in real life. In the ongoing discussions about what is and is not appropriate for worship, sometimes the disagreement itself is expressed in intentionally dramatic terms. In Aiden Kavanagh's classic volume on liturgical renewal, *Elements of Rite*, a critical chapter is devoted to what he calls the elementary rules of liturgical usage. In it, he argues that churches should not be carpeted, lest they be

> too soft for the liturgy, which needs hardness, sonority, and a certain bracing discomfort much like the Gospel itself. Liturgical ambience must challenge, for one comes to the liturgy to transact the public business of death and life rather than to be tucked in with fables and featherpuffs.[13]

Declaring that the furniture in a worship space should be both significant and kept to a minimum, he insists:

> Pews, which entered liturgical place only recently, nail the assembly down, proclaiming that the liturgy is not a common action but a preachment perpetrated upon the seated, an ecclesiastical opera

13. Kavanagh, *Elements*, 21.

done by virtuosi for a paying audience. Pews distance the congregation, disenfranchise the faithful, and rend the assembly. Filling a church with immovable pews is similar to placing bleachers directly on a basketball court: it not only interferes with movement but changes the event into something else entirely.[14]

Kavanagh does not use words like "entertainment," "theater," or even "drama" in his critique of late-twentieth-century worship. However, it is clear that he has something like these in mind when he writes:

> It may be profitable to consider the effects which the immobilization of the assembly, caused by the proliferation of pews, has had on liturgical speech (the modes of prayer and declamation) and on liturgical music once these are allowed to develop without fundamental reference to ceremonial movement. Liturgical speech then functions less to organize and direct a public assembly toward its common and objective purpose; it functions more to address individuals sitting in place and having the leisure to reflect on their own subjectivity. Liturgical music then functions as a set-piece for appreciation by intently listening audiences, and textual meaning becomes overshadowed by compositional and performative virtuosity; it is no longer music to move by—"parade" music, simple and rhythmic—but music to listen to.[15]

Putting aside the fact that pews were an invention of the Reformation, which can hardly be considered recent, and virtuoso church music has existed at least as long, Kavanagh is concerned that sitting still instead of being free to gather around the font, pulpit, or altar changes worship from a participatory event where everyone has a role into a theatrical event presented for the purpose of aesthetic contemplation. While his concerns are worthy of consideration (even if hyperbolically expressed), there is a long history of comparing, or even conflating, worship and theater, stretching back at least to the fourth-century travels of Egeria. More recently, books such as Patricia Wilson-Kastner's *Sacred Drama: A Spirituality of Christian Liturgy*, published in 1999; Timothy Radcliffe's *Why Go to Church? The Drama of the Eucharist*, which was the Archbishop of Canterbury's Lent Book for 2009; Roger Grainger's *The Drama of the Rite: Worship, Liturgy and Theatre Performance*, also published in 2009; and many other books

---

14. Kavanagh, *Elements*, 22.
15. Kavanagh, *Elements*, 37–38.

and articles lead the reader to expect similarities between worship and the dramatic arts.

Wilson-Kastner argues that drama is a useful descriptor for liturgy, particularly in the sense of being a representation or mimesis of life. She does note that drama as a metaphor for liturgy is not well received by many liturgists today, particularly citing Gordon Lathrop, who would prefer to consider liturgy as the weaving together of people, things, actions, and words into patterns of meaning.[16] Nevertheless, she defends the dramatic metaphor because both liturgy and drama use the obvious elements of players, costumes, and plot, and, more importantly, because liturgy is a dramatic action of the community. Calling liturgy mimesis—imitation—of life, and a cosmic, comic, cultic drama, she says that it is formed as a sacrificial meal in which everyone participates:

> The liturgy is always formed as mimetic drama. In the Eucharist, we bring the whole human condition before God—our history, our temptations, the good we do, our needs, our hopes, our fears. Each time we participate, the drama is a bit different, the focus is slightly changed—different liturgical seasons, different readings, new people, individual experiences, community changes—and all the elements add new dimension to the greatest drama of all.
>
> In the Eucharist, we remember God's creation of the world, our alienation, and our restoration in Christ through the Spirit. . . . Each time the liturgical drama is performed, at least two key dimensions are present: The fundamental great action of human life is enacted, and unique lives are expressed in the liturgy. . . . Liturgy is not timeless and static. Each generation, each performance offers a different Hamlet or Electra, with a different vision and ever new revelations.[17]

Drawing out the dramatic metaphor even further, Wilson-Kastner notes that every congregation or gathering has its own expectations, so behaviors and even words that are appropriate and expected in a revival might be quite different from those in a Quaker meeting. What is important, she writes, is that ritual itself is fundamentally dramatic, and just as in any given instance of a play by Shakespeare,

> the acts, the words, the interweaving of the elements are expected by the participants in the drama. They are expected to be in a

16. Wilson-Kastner, *Sacred Drama*, 12.
17. Wilson-Kastner, *Sacred Drama*, 14.

recognizable form because the liturgy is integral and essential to forming and nurturing our identity. . . . By sharing regularly in the same cultic rituals and symbols, the community continually reinforces in its members the sense of all being participants. Sometimes what appears to be a small aspect of the liturgy as cult is important to a participant because it is that person's role in the drama. To change the cultic form is to challenge the person's part in the play and the outcome of the drama.[18]

This is not to say that the script cannot be revised or that individuals cannot take on different roles over time. The author gives as an example the change in the Episcopal practice of Maundy Thursday from simply reading particular scriptural passages for the Eucharist to actual foot-washing within the worshipping assembly.[19]

Wilson-Kastner goes on to use the metaphor of drama in discussing the connection of liturgy to the entire cosmic scope of creation, good and evil, and the entirety of the sacred:

Our liturgy expands the context and the participants well beyond the human struggle with ourselves, our feelings, our desires, to embrace the entire universe. The players in the drama include God, angelic and demonic powers, humanity and its world, and all the rest of creation, focused in the church, who is, if you will, producing the drama. Sometimes this cosmic scope is explicit, other times implicit, but it is always present.[20]

At this point, she shifts from defending the metaphor to simply using it, moving further and further away from the particularities of drama as theater to a different use of the word that asserts that this or that element of liturgy is inherently dramatic.

Similarly, Timothy Radcliffe explicitly encourages Christians to understand the Eucharistic liturgy as a three-act play. While cautioning against expecting a big, showy, emotional experience, he nonetheless labels each chapter by act and scene number, urging readers to see that

the Eucharist is a drama in three acts, through which we share God's life and begin even now to be touched by God's happiness. Each act prepares for the next. By listening to the word of God, we grow in faith and so become ready to proclaim the Creed and

18. Wilson-Kastner, *Sacred Drama*, 15.

19. Wilson-Kastner, *Sacred Drama*, 16.

20. Wilson-Kastner, *Sacred Drama*, 17.

ask for what we need. In the second act, belief leads to hope. From the preparation of gifts to the end of the Eucharistic Prayer, we remember how on the night before he died Jesus took bread, blessed it and gave it to the disciples saying, "This is my body, given for you." Faced with failure, violence and death, we are given hope, repeating Christ's own prayer. In the final act, from the "Our Father" onwards, our hope culminates in love. We prepare for Communion. We encounter the risen Christ and his victory over death and hatred and receive the bread of life. Finally we are sent on our way—"Go and serve the Lord"—as a sign of God's love for the world.[21]

For Radcliffe, the Eucharist enacts the fundamental drama of being human, and forms us as people who are at home with God, deeply imbued with the theological virtues of faith, hope, and charity.[22] Like Wilson-Kastner, Radcliffe defines drama differently than one might when speaking of theatrical productions. Indeed, he makes that very point:

> Going to the Eucharist is not like going to see a film. One can come straight off the street into a cinema and be bowled over by a drama on the screen. One is caught up in a story which begins and ends within a couple of hours. But the Eucharist is the drama of one's whole life—birth to death and beyond. It reshapes one's heart and mind as someone whose happiness is to be found in God.[23]

If the Eucharistic drama is approached as a form of entertainment, in competition with television or sports or movies, Radcliffe warns, there is the danger that both congregation and clergy will think it is the clergy's job to put on a good show.

Roger Grainger likewise sees certain similarities between worship and theater, not least among them that each "first of all makes its own world, then transports us beyond it."[24]

> Liturgy's purpose is to have a transforming effect on the lives of those involved. No wonder, then, that its action is dramatic in the sense that it resembles an actual piece of theatre. . . . Ritual and theatre have this in common: that they counteract the human tendency to include otherness within the self by regarding it as

21. Radcliffe, *Why Go*, 7.
22. Radcliffe, *Why Go*, 7.
23. Radcliffe, *Why Go*, 8.
24. Grainger, *Drama*, 9.

an idea to be woven into the pattern of thought, filed alongside every other idea, and treat it as a real presence—the presence of a beckoning absence, a gap which can only be filled by personal relationship, the experience of reaching across to the Other.[25]

For Grainger, the difference between worship or ritual and theater lies in the subject matter:

> The drama sets out to portray life, while ritual mirrors the perfection of the Infinite. In this sense then the real subject matter of ritual lies beyond the everyday experiences of living—the subject matter, that is, not its effects as we are drawn into the sphere of beyondness by paying attention with our whole selves in acts of worship.[26]

Unlike Radcliffe, who understands the drama of the liturgy as unfolding within the relatively unchanging Roman Catholic tradition, Grainger sees ritual as akin to an experimental workshop in which the story of God's relationship with humans may be told in many different ways. Indeed, most of Grainger's book recounts various gatherings in which members of his congregation create ad hoc rituals in response to particular situations in their lives. One of these involved a man whom Grainger calls Simon, who told a church discussion group about his inability to express his grief over the death of his father many years earlier. Using processes that actors refer to as "theater games," the participants

> exchanged letters with people in their own life stories who they were longing to hear from and to whom they had some things vitally important to say; later on the letters "became" the people themselves as individual dramas were improvised and the workshop began to move into another phase.[27]

Eventually, they began to act out the story of Simon and his father:

> Although this was played as a drama it was not, in the usual sense of the word, *dramatic*. In fact the whole episode was tentative and low key out of respect for Simon's feelings. . . . Later on, during the Memorial Liturgy for Simon's Father, celebrated in church later the

---

25. Grainger, *Drama*, 17.

26. Grainger, *Drama*, 24.

27. Grainger, *Drama*, 63.

same week . . . his control gave way and against all his principles
(and those of his father), Simon wept. [28]

Grainger gives the order of worship for the memorial liturgy, which on
the page seems to have been a relatively unremarkable Protestant service.
He then sums up the entire sequence of events, including the discussion
in the group, the re-enactment of Simon's story, and the ensuing liturgy,
concluding:

> This, then, is *the drama of the rite* [italics in original]—the cho-
> sen mode of God's revelation, the inclusive-exclusive event; not
> a message but a happening, a divine play which calls upon a sa-
> cred history but is itself a living presence, the scenario of ultimate
> transformation.[29]

While Grainger does not seem to mean the same thing by the word
"rite" that Radcliffe does, there is clearly something about ritual in general, and Christian worship in particular, that compels the comparison to
theater.

Entertainment

That people have deeply spiritual experiences at concerts, plays, movies,
and even dances is not a new observation. Neither is it a new idea that at
least some parts of church services are and should be entertaining. Nevertheless, many people struggle with the notion that the church has anything
to learn from the world of entertainment. What is it about entertainment
that causes so much unease?

In 1985, Neil Postman wrote a book called *Amusing Ourselves to
Death: Public Discourse in the Age of Show Business*. In it, he argued that
the move from books and newspapers to television "has dramatically and
irreversibly shifted the content and meaning of public discourse, since two
media so vastly different cannot accommodate the same ideas."[30] Lament-
ing the loss of what he understood as rational discussion in public media, he contends "under the governance of the printing press, discourse
in America was different from what it is now—generally coherent, serious
and rational; and then how, under the governance of television, it has be-

28. Grainger, *Drama*, 63–64.

29. Grainger, *Drama*, 74.

30. Postman, *Amusing Ourselves*, 8.

come shriveled and absurd," resulting in "the content of much of our public discourse [becoming] dangerous nonsense."[31]

While the title of Postman's book used the word "amusing," it is clear throughout that the author equates amusement with entertainment. Most of his discussion depends on an unstated and unexamined assumption that philosophical argument is the apex of human discourse, whereas that which appeals to the emotions is somehow suspect. While that may be true when making public policy decisions, which was the primary area of Postman's concern, other values are equally if not more important in Christian worship. Today, the kind of reasoned argument that was taught in the homiletics departments of the major seminaries at the time Postman was writing has been largely supplanted by more narrative, contextual styles that appeal to the emotions as much as to the intellect, not because we want to be "amused" in church, but because human beings are more than just intellect. Indeed, some communities of faith have always known this. As homiletics professor Cleophus Larue says:

> We have always known that there is more to the preaching life than the realities of the empirical world that we can see and touch. We have always known there is more to preaching than interpretive strategies and correct biblical exegesis. In dealing with mystery there are other dimensions that simply cannot be accounted for even when you have followed every step of the exegesis process.[32]

Nevertheless, Postman's assertion that we as a society are amusing ourselves to death remains a frequent touchstone in discussions of how Christian worship should be conducted. An underlying suspicion of imaginative, emotional, and physical engagement with the holy, rather than intellectual assent to propositional truths, continues to be an important strand in much of the theological academy as well as the church at large.

As Heather Murray Elkins pointed out toward the beginning of this book, the word "entertainment" may be used in a variety of ways. We entertain dinner guests; we entertain ideas; we entertain ourselves with video games and internet surfing to fill up otherwise boring moments. The word suggests amusement or enjoyment, and dictionaries suggest as synonyms words like "pleasure," "leisure," "recreation," "relaxation," "fun," "enjoyment," "interest," or "diversion." An entertainment might be any kind of event or performance, especially those that might be described as a

31. Postman, *Amusing Ourselves*, 16.
32. LaRue, *Believe I'll Testify*, 54.

spectacle, extravaganza, or pageant. Biblical storyteller Dennis Dewey offers a different vision:

> Look at the etymology of the word *entertain*. It comes from *inter*
> + *tenere* and means "to draw in." I think there is good theological
> sense behind our engaging in a communicative act that draws not
> only teller and listener together, but binds them in a living tether
> with the sound-and-breath story that has been told, heard, retold,
> heard again and traditioned to us by a glorious cloud of witnesses.
> What could be better worship or education than that which finds
> teller, listeners, the communion of saints, and the God whose story
> is told all bound together in a sacramental moment of experience?
> Now THAT'S entertainment![33]

Despite Dewey's passionate attempt to rehabilitate the word, entertainment continues to suggest frivolity or lack of serious intent. For many, to call something an entertainment suggests a certain pejorative critique, a sense that there is something not quite proper with such enjoyment. Indeed, at various times and places, dancing, movies, circuses, rock music, and other activities were considered not simply foolish time-wasters, but sinful. This pejorative sense is generally uppermost in the minds of those who criticize certain church practices as entertainment. For some, there is a sense that a worship service should be serious, solemn, even somber, and that the laughter or applause that are characteristic of entertainment have no place in the devotion that is offered to God.

For others, this distinction is not so clear. As Janet Walton tells the story, someone at an orientation event for new students

> pointed out that it was really a disorientation service that students
> go through, because we are trying not to orient them, but to let go
> and interrupt their lives and raise something new. We created the
> yellow brick road from *The Wizard of Oz*. People hear that and
> say, "this is really entertainment." But it wasn't about that. It was
> about making another connection with people that was real. This
> was a connection that got under their skin quite easily, and then
> they could rest and trust us. We were doing something that was
> humanly entertaining, but really what we wanted was something
> humanly connecting.[34]

---

33. Dewey, "That's Entertainment."

34. Walton, interview.

This human connection is at the heart of true worship as well as much that is categorized as entertainment. It is clear that entertainment has more ability to make human connections than is acknowledged by the dismissive term "mere entertainment." When popular films based on comic books such as *Black Panther* or *Wonder Woman* can be described as "imperative viewing as both pop-culture events and paradigm shifts," which to ignore "would have been to opt out of the conversational zeitgeist, declare sociocultural illiteracy, surrender one's own claim to relevance,"[35] something more important is going on than simple diversion.

People want to connect to stories that are bigger than their own individual lives, stories that connect them with the past and the future and with one another. For the students who were disoriented in a worship service featuring a yellow brick road, the connection to countless childhood viewings of the *Wizard of Oz* helped them connect to one another at the beginning of their seminary journey. Similarly, new myths about a technological utopia called Wakanda hidden deep in the African countryside, or a woman warrior who can compel men to tell the truth, leap unscathed from exploding buildings, and stop bullets with her magical bracelets, help individuals make connections with others who share their hopes and dreams of a better future.

Certainly, many entertainers can be crude or mean-spirited, playing to the basest emotions and motives of their audiences, rather than holding up examples of courage, inclusion, or compassion. It is also true that much that is called worship or liturgy can be equally divisive or offensive, validating the exclusive or elitist tendencies of worshipers rather than reminding them of the eternal outpouring of love and grace that God offers to all. Entertainment can be mindless; worship can be boring. Both worship and entertainment can be self-serving, self-congratulatory, unaware, and unwilling to become anything more than a way to pass the time. To compare the worst of entertainment with the best of worship, or the other way around, is to do both a disservice.

Excellence

At its simplest, excellence is the quality of doing something particularly well. In the interviews, Ruth Duck, Eileen Guenther, and Geoffrey Moore all insist that excellence is crucially important for good worship. Excellence,

35. Hornaday, "What Defines."

however, can take many forms. David O. Taylor tells the story about a woman in his childhood church in Guatemala who liked to sing. She would stand up in the midst of the congregation and declaim,

> "I don't know how to read. I don't know how to sing. I don't know how to play. But for the glory of God!" . . . And that is precisely what we got: a poorly played, poorly sung musical piece that strangled our ability to perceive any trace of God's glory. We loved her dearly, and there was no doubt that her heart was in the right place. But her actions betrayed a dismissive view of art that revealed something of her view about God. And, I submit, there is no evidence in Scripture that God pits the sincerity of our hearts over the excellency of artmaking.[36]

Taylor goes on to argue that there is place in worship for simple art, but that it is also important to differentiate between good art and bad. It is clear that he is both struggling to uphold the value of artistic expertise and to welcome the whole-hearted participation of the entire congregation. As an artist, he encourages other artists to keep making excellent artwork because the world needs it, but as a pastor he recognizes that there are times in the life of the church when a different understanding of "excellence" is needed. Citing his admiration for professional modern dance and his impatience with "glittery, satiny 'praise dancing,'" he writes:

> I also realize that sometimes we as a congregation need, for example, to let our children dance before us. They will be anything but nuanced, and some kid will make faces at his mother while another dances to the beat in her own head.[37]

Taylor is attempting to articulate a definition of excellence that does not necessarily depend upon the constant striving for perfection or what Eileen Guenther describes as "the desire for pure vowels and a sound that sounds like a single singer even though there are fifty singers."[38] Like Guenther, who noted that a singer who may not have a wonderful voice but has a wonderful spirit can move a congregation to tears, Taylor admonishes his readers:

> But occasionally we need to remember that the kingdom of God does not belong only to adults. Even as we witness unpolished

---

36. Taylor, "The Dangers," in Taylor, *For the Beauty*, 150.
37. Taylor, "The Dangers," in Taylor, *For the Beauty*, 158.
38. Guenther, interview, 2016.

dancing, here in our corporate gathering, we will be reminded that our goal as Christians is not to be polished and impressive, but to be true. The children dancing before the God who in Jesus of Nazareth pulls the little ones into the middle of his preaching reminds us that we are all clumsy, unhinged humans. We too step on others' toes. We too need grace. So the kids' dance becomes not an interruption to the "serious" work of the pastor, but rather an occasion for the gospel to penetrate our hearts with truth.[39]

Even so, there is a place for the kind of polish and skill that only years of intentional practice can produce. In upholding the glorious chaos of children dancing before God, Taylor does not quite engage the problem of what (if anything) to do about the unskilled singer who believed she had heard God's voice telling her to do something creative but did not have sufficient skill to do it excellently. As Taylor points out, this poses a problem for those who plan and lead worship yet want to be gracious and loving to every member of the congregation. As Dale Savidge writes:

> "God gave me this play" can be an expression of sincere intention, or it can be a mask for shoddy craftsmanship. God's leading is never apart from God's attributes of beauty and excellence. If God gives an artist a work to produce, God always expects the artist to use, attain, or hire the skills necessary to create the work with excellence—this is the way God created the world and that is the pattern God has set for us. It would be absurd for a musical composer to claim divine impetus for a piano sonata apart from training in musical composition and theory. Similarly, a writer must make the sacrifices necessary to learn the technique of playwriting and couple that with the leading of the Holy Spirit.[40]

In *Performer as Priest and Prophet*, Judith Rock and Norman Mealy write of the intense loneliness and self-doubt that many artists experience:

> Many hours each week are spent in solitary practice as the musician confronts self-limitation and -worth. Doubt assails that person from all directions. "Will I ever be able to play this? Why can't I keep a steady beat? Do I really know what this music is all about? Will I ever fully understand it? Are my choices the right ones? What is 'right?'"[41]

---

39. Taylor, "The Dangers," in Taylor, *For the Beauty*, 158.
40. Savidge, "The Christian at Work," in Johnson and Savidge, *Performing*, 103.
41. Rock and Mealy, *Performer*, 74.

Like well-trained preachers and liturgists, skilled dancers and musicians are able to articulate prophetic and priestly vision through the skills that they have acquired as a result of this persistent practice, skills that would not be available to the congregation in any other way:

> Technical dance training is not necessary for congregational movement or, for example, movement used within a prayer group as part of its meditation together. But training is essential for most dance done to be watched, in the church as well as in the theater, for the amateur as well as the professional. The dancer as performer is one who subordinates the self to the art of dancing, serving choreographic and technical forms so that communication can take place through a disciplined, articulate body. . . . Technique is essential, because the point of performance is not self-expression, the giving of the self to the watchers; the point is the giving of the *dance* [emphasis in original] to the watchers. Neither in the theater nor in the church can one get by on sincerity.[42]

While sincerity cannot replace technical skill, neither can technical skill replace authenticity. The sound of congregational song, in which someone is always off-key and someone else is always a little ahead of the beat, has a different kind of excellence than that of a well-trained choir. The spontaneous swaying and dancing in the aisles that breaks out when the musicians hit a certain groove has different kind of excellence than that of a carefully choreographed liturgical dance. The enthusiastic song and dance of the inspired but untutored has one kind of excellence, and the performance of the skilled musician or dancer has another. Perhaps both are needed for the full excellence of the Body of Christ.

Liturgy

For many Christians, the words "liturgy" and "worship" are essentially synonymous. Others, however, differentiate strongly between them, reserving "liturgy" to refer to formal, heavily scripted services which rely on prayer books and rubrics, such as might be found in Roman Catholic, Eastern Orthodox, and Episcopalian or Lutheran services. In this way of speaking, "worship" is used for the somewhat less formal gatherings typically found in the frontier or revival tradition, where there may not even be a printed bulletin for the congregation to follow the order of service.

42. Rock and Mealy, *Performer*, 80.

The original Greek source, *leiturgia,* was used to refer to what might be called "public works," things like road-building or garbage collection. Later, *leiturgia* came to be associated with religious activities because, like building a road for all to use, it was work that belonged to everyone but was actually done only by a few on behalf of the many. However, etymology can only go so far in explaining what a word means today. As liturgical scholar John Burkhart notes, just as words in English acquire new meanings and uses, the meaning of Greek words associated with worship changed over time. Looking at various uses of the word in the New Testament, he writes:

> *Leiturgia,* which had meant public service, a work done for the people, and had come to mean cultic activities for the gods of civil religion, became among Christians charitable good works, such as the alms collected for the poor within the congregation at Jerusalem (Rom. 15:27) or the missionary ministry of sharing the gospel with the Gentiles (Rom. 15:16). Only in Acts 13:2 is the corresponding verb (*leitourgeo*) used for Christian worship.[43]

Others have argued that since *leiturgia* may be translated as "the work of the people," it should be understood as the work that is done by the people as a whole, rather than what is done on their behalf. This distinction is, in itself, important, because whether one thinks of liturgy being done *by* the people or by someone else *on behalf of* them makes a big difference to the understanding of what should happen when Christians gather to worship God.

Over time, liturgy has come to have several different but overlapping meanings. Some scholars use the term to refer to specific texts and rubrics, whether in ancient manuscripts or contemporary liturgical books. Others appear to use it more generally, almost like a Platonic ideal, of which any given text is but an exemplar. And still others refer not to the text at all, but to its enactment. For instance, Orthodox Christians refer to going to church on Sunday as attending the Divine Liturgy. Roman Catholics talk about the first part of a gathering for worship, up to and including the homily, as the Liturgy of the Word; the second part is called the Eucharistic Liturgy. Various other denominational bodies also follow this practice, often replacing "Eucharistic Liturgy" with "Liturgy of the Table." In general, however, Protestants more frequently speak of going to worship (or just going to church) than going to a liturgy.

---

43. Burkhart, *Worship,* 20–21.

Play

Play, like entertainment, is often absent from any talk about what is supposed to happen in church. Play is what children do and has no place in the serious business of worshipping God. Unfortunately, for many, worship is just one more thing on the to-do list. In this way of thinking, reading scripture aloud for the congregation or singing in the choir is just another task to be completed rather than an occasion for joyful participation. Philosopher David Applebaum notes that we have allowed so much of what we do to fall under the banner of accomplishment that our vision

> has narrowed to that of efficient producers as we go about remaking our planet's face in our self-image. As we lean further over the abyss, we come closer to a reflection of ourselves in these dark waters: a being hellbent on controlling its own destiny. Around us, nature gently and not so gently objects.[44]

Play, Applebaum reminds his readers, is spontaneous. While worship is usually more planned than play, worship at its best is like play in having no ulterior motive, no reason to exist other than the enjoyment of this unrepeatable moment:

> Here, with fresh eyes to see and ears to hear we can take ourselves in again and be nourished. Serious, frivolous, absorbing, dismaying, or satisfying, play restores an impulse to live in search of openness. It restores us to the essential questions.[45]

In "What 'Play' Is," an extract from *Homo Ludens: A Study of the Play-Element in Culture*, Johan Huizinga reminds the reader that even animals play. Therefore, he asserts, play is older than culture, although many of its expressions in humans are culturally bound. Play, he argues,

> is more than a mere physiological phenomenon or psychological reflex. It goes beyond the confines of purely physical or purely biological activity. It is a *significant* [emphasis in original] function— that is to say, there is some sense to it. In play there is something "at play" which transcends the immediate needs of life and imparts meaning to the action. All play means something.[46]

---

44. Applebaum, "Focus," 1.
45. Applebaum, "Focus," 1.
46. Huizinga, "What 'Play' Is," 59.

The essence of play is freedom and cannot be coerced. Children and animals play because they enjoy doing so. Adults, on the other hand, often think of play as superfluous, unnecessary, something to be done only when the chores are done. Only "when play is a recognized cultural function—a rite, a ceremony—is it bound up with notions of obligation and duty."[47]

There are many similarities between play and worship. Both, for instance, are understood as different in some important way from ordinary life. Like worship,

> play is not "ordinary" or "real" life. It is rather a stepping out of "real" life into a temporary sphere of activity with a disposition all its own. Every child knows perfectly well that he is "only pretending" or that it was "only for fun." . . . This "only pretending" quality of play betrays a consciousness of the inferiority of play compared with "seriousness," a feeling that seems to be something as primary as play itself. Nevertheless . . . the consciousness of play being "only a pretend" does not by any means prevent it from proceeding with the utmost seriousness, with an absorption, a devotion that passes into rapture and temporarily at least, completely abolishes that troublesome "only" feeling. Any game can at any time wholly run away with the players.[48]

This description of play could also describe worship at its best. In addition, play, like most services of Christian worship, is limited in duration and place. Both begin at a set time, play themselves out, and come to an end. Some forms of play, like games or rituals or music, become fixed as a cultural phenomenon. Repetition, whether as repeated instances or as a repeated element within the form, is, Huizinga asserts, one of the most essential qualities of play. Similarly, he notes, all play

> moves and has its being within a playground marked off beforehand either materially or ideally, deliberately or as a matter of course. Just as there is no formal difference between play and ritual, so the "consecrated spot" cannot be formally distinguished from the play-ground. The arena, the card-table, the magic circle, the temple, the stage, the screen, the tennis court, the court of justice, etc., are all in form and function play-grounds, i.e., forbidden spots, hallowed, within which special rules obtain. All are

47. Huizinga, "What 'Play' Is," 60.
48. Huizinga, "What 'Play' Is," 60.

temporary worlds within the ordinary world, dedicated to the performance of an act apart.[49]

Similarly, worship can create a temporary world within the ordinary world, allowing those present to separate themselves from the ordinary cares and activities that keep them preoccupied with goals and accomplishments. Just as there is no goal in play except the enjoyment of the game, there is no goal to worship except the enjoyment of being in God's presence.

Prayer

Prayer is central to Christian worship. Sometimes prayers are offered by whoever is leading the service, or by individual members of the congregation. Other times they are spoken responsively or in unison by the congregation. Prayers can be sung or chanted or held in silence. In some traditions, the prayers to be spoken on any given occasion are prescribed by the denomination, while in others, only extemporaneous prayers are believed to come from the heart. Christians pray for forgiveness and for healing; they pray in thanksgiving and praise, and in supplication and intercession. Prayer often takes the formal shape of a collect, beginning with an address to God, followed by the subject of the prayer, and closing with a doxology, or it can be more free-form, moving from subject to subject as the one who is praying sees fit.

It is hard to imagine any service of Christian worship without prayer. Even so, people sometimes disagree about what prayer is. For some, prayer is talking to God, telling God what is on their minds and in their hearts. For others, prayer is a kind of listening, of waiting quietly so that God can speak to them in the silence. Still others dance or paint their prayers or write them as poems.

In *Movies Are Prayers: How Films Voice Our Deepest Longings*, film critic Josh Larsen posits that prayer is the natural, human response to situations that evoke awe, anger, confusion, or other big emotions.[50] While making careful distinctions between organized Christian liturgy and the social conventions of going to the movies, he also notes the architectural similarities of many churches and movie theaters, as well as the many venues in which people pray outside of church or at other times that are set aside for

49. Huizinga, "What 'Play' Is," 62.

50. Larsen, *Movies Are Prayers*, 6.

that activity. Larsen cites a description of prayer by Theophan the Recluse, a Russian Orthodox bishop who lived in the nineteenth century: "Prayer is the raising of the mind and heart to God—for praise and thanksgiving and beseeching [God] for the good things necessary for soul and body."[51] Larsen celebrates the mixture of heart and mind, intellect and emotion, implicit in Theophan's description:

> Prayer also takes place beyond the boundary waters, in places and ways we might not expect. This human instinct to reach out in praise or lament or supplication or confession to the divine does not take place only in church, guided by liturgy and pastors. It isn't limited to early morning devotions, in that serene space before silence gives way to the day. It isn't strictly the domain of dinner tables, where families gather to recite familiar words ("God is great, God is good . . ."). And it isn't an instinct shared only by Christians. Prayer can be expressed by anyone and can take place everywhere. Even in movie theaters.[52]

While Larsen is neither a theologian nor a liturgist, he makes important observations about the ways that movies reveal the hopes and desires of the cinematographers, editors, actors, directors, musicians, production designers, and other artists who work together collaboratively to make movies that will be available for audiences to while away a couple of otherwise empty hours. As Larsen makes clear, it takes the efforts of hundreds or even thousands of real people to make the movies that so many others take for granted. And "when the resulting movies genuinely yearn, mournfully lament, fitfully rage, honestly confess, or joyously celebrate, they serve as prayers."[53]

Larsen is not, of course, suggesting that showing a movie in church should replace the specific prayers of confession, thanksgiving, and supplication that are integral to virtually all worshipping traditions. Rather, he is inviting his readers to acknowledge the very real yearnings that lead people to make all kinds of movies, even those that are routinely dismissed as mere entertainment. In a larger sense, this is an invitation to those who spend an hour or two in intentional worship on most Sunday mornings to

51. Larsen, *Movies Are Prayers*, 7. Larsen gives the following citation: "Theophan the Recluse, quoted in *Philokalia: The Easter Christian Spiritual Texts*, trans. G.E.H. Palmer, Philp Sherrard, and Kallistos Ware; annotated by Allyne Smith (Woodstock, VT: Skylight Paths, 2006), 32."

52. Larsen, *Movies Are Prayers*, 7.

53. Larsen, *Movies Are Prayers*, 12.

remember that God loves the world, not just the people who go to church. In this inclusive vision,

> movies, at their most potent, are not diversions or products or even works of art, but prayerful gestures received by God. . . . We best honor movies when we allow them this potential, rather than treat them like ways to pass the time or purchases to be made or unwashed items to be dissected according to an arbitrary moral code; and . . . no matter what our response, God still watches them with a heart that is both righteous and merciful.[54]

It is not only movies that are prayers. So are all sorts of games, books, songs, dances, plays, paintings, and the many other creative productions that human beings make with integrity and passion. Just as the Word of God is more than words, the prayers of the world are more than what happens when someone says, "Let us pray."

Production Values

Despite the unease at what is often dismissed as merely entertainment, people go on having deeply spiritual experiences at movies, rock concerts, and even the circus. That, in part, is behind the attempts of some churches to attend to what in the entertainment world is termed "production values." Production values are things like lighting, staging, sightlines, and acoustics—in other words, all the things that, for instance, make the difference between a big-budget film and a low-cost indie.

In the church world, one might say that the proverbial small country church, with five quavering voices in the choir, amplification that often emits the familiar high squeal of feedback, and a casual worship style, has low production values; while the Episcopal cathedral found in any major city, with its highly trained choir, carefully calibrated sound system, and close adherence to the rubrics of the Book of Common Prayer, has high production values.

Similarly, a mega-church typically has high production values, albeit in a different style. The well-equipped mega-church features a stage rather than a pulpit, an amplified praise band rather than a choir and organ or piano. Well-designed visuals are projected on screens that take the place of both stained glass and hymnals or prayer books. These high production

54. Larsen, *Movies Are Prayers*, 179–80.

values draw in many people who are put off by the offhand, slipshod look of many smaller churches. At the same time, these same high production values are what sometimes makes worship in a mega-church look and feel to some with other tastes much more like a Saturday night concert than Sunday morning worship.

Ritual

"Ritual" is another word that is often problematic. Dictionaries define ritual as a set of actions, often accompanied by prescribed words, performed according to a set order. While many who study rituals describe them as unchangeable, others may have a more elastic view, noting that rituals often change from one instance to another, and that new rituals arise in response to new circumstances. In her groundbreaking book *Ritual Theory, Ritual Practice*, Catherine Bell refuses to define the word "ritual" at all, preferring the term "ritualization." For Bell, "ritualization" means

> various culturally-specific strategies for setting some activities off from others, for creating and privileging a qualitative distinction between the "sacred" and the "profane," and for ascribing such distinctions to realities thought to transcend the powers of human actors.[55]

Thus, the ritual of Holy Communion is made different from ordinary eating and drinking by saying special words, using special utensils, and making special gestures, as well as by the belief that God enters into the ritual in a way that differs from God's presence at other times and places. Similarly, the ritual of baptism is not the same as ordinary bathing or washing, but rather involves particular words and gestures, as well as (in some cases) special clothing or special objects that are only used in this situation.

While Roman Catholics, Orthodox Christians, Episcopalians, and Lutherans have always had a deep respect for the ritual aspects of worship, Protestant groups that trace their lineage through Calvin or the radical reformers are often suspicious of their power and efficacy, dismissing them as "mere ritual." This suspicion is a legacy of the Reformation and the Enlightenment, in which most Roman Catholic norms were called into question by those who held new ideas and ideals. As Richard Muir writes in his recent volume *Ritual in Early Modern Europe*:

55. Bell, *Ritual Theory*, 74.

By the eighteenth century, "ritual" had become a dirty word. Like rhetoric, that other great interest of the Renaissance, ritual came to imply insincerity and empty formality, the very antithesis of the Enlightenment that prized individual sincerity and authenticity. How did it happen that what had been the path to God in the medieval period had for many people become a pernicious form of deception by the early modern period?[56]

Muir explains that this transition originated in the sixteenth-century Reformation, when ritual was greatly simplified and reimagined as memorial rather than sacrament. The Reformation shifted attention from the emotive power of rituals to questions about their meaning. The eighteenth-century Enlightenment deepened this suspicion of anything that could not be explained. In this new emphasis on meaning, ritual was often dismissed as not only an unnecessary part of worship but an actual impediment to faith. However, as religious rituals fell into disfavor, secular ones continued to flourish:

> Modern rationalists have even imagined themselves to be above the delusions and obscurantism of religious rituals, even as they are oblivious to the secular rituals in which they participate. The rituals of modern mass culture have created a shifting and transient sense of the sacred, now invested in the political ideology of the moment, romantic love of nature, charismatic leaders, jingoistic nationalism, idealized domesticity, or endless cults, fads, [and] ephemera.[57]

In the latter part of the twentieth century, a new suspicion of Enlightenment thinking arose in many parts of Western society, leading to the appropriation by other groups of the rituals of Native Americans and other indigenous peoples; attempts to revive European paganism in the form of Wicca and other practices; and the invention of new rituals by certain groups of feminists and the men's consciousness movement. In this atmosphere of renewed interest in the uses of ritual, the liturgical renewal movement that began in the Roman Catholic Church caught the attention of many Protestants. As Catherine Bell notes:

> Ritual is never simply or solely a matter of routine, habit, or "the dead weight of tradition." Indeed, routinization and habitualization may be strategies in certain cultural situations, but so might

56. Muir, *Ritual*, 294.
57. Muir, *Ritual*, 299.

the infrequent yet periodic reproduction of a complex ritual tradition.[58]

The Second Vatican Council affected not only the Roman Catholic Church, but most of the mainline Protestant denominations. In its wake, both Catholics and Protestants rewrote their hymnals and books of worship, taking into account a newfound understanding that ritual is not about what can be said in prose, but rather about entering an as-if world in which we ask and answer questions that cannot be addressed in any other way. While many Protestants still tend to over explain what they do and why they do it, there is an increasing respect for the deep, relatively wordless power of rituals. In many Protestant churches today, it is not uncommon to celebrate communion as an intrinsic part of every Sunday service, holding up and visibly breaking a whole loaf of bread. Rituals that once were shunned as "too Catholic" are now common among Protestants. In both Protestant and Roman Catholic churches, copious amounts of water may be used for baptisms that take place in the midst of the congregation rather than in private. Both Protestant and Roman Catholic congregations dramatically observe the beginning of Lent by marking participants' foreheads with ashes made from the palms carried in last year's Palm/Passion Sunday procession. For many, ritual no longer suggests empty repetition, but rather the deep familiarity and comfort of regular gatherings with friends over food and drink; of endless summer days at the beach, swimming out over and over again to ride the next wave onto the sand; or of bedtime stories repeated so often that everyone knows all the words by heart yet still begs to hear them once again.

There is a deep connection between ritual and play. Tom Driver discusses the way that humans learn to move from incoherent babbling to speaking a particular language, as an example of this connection:

> If we did not first babble and cry like babies, we would not later talk. One piece of evidence is that the babbling and crying stage is not entirely left behind as speech matures, but remains in the background of all later articulation. To have a good feel for any human voice that addresses us, we must have some intuition of the cries and babbles out of which it has arisen and to which it has the possibility at any moment to return. The same holds for language's other behavioral roots, the repertoire of "body language" with which the child, like the kitten, plays and becomes expressive.

58. Bell, *Ritual Theory*, 92.

One function of play is to experiment—to produce and reproduce, invent, and repeat, try things this way and that until a response, either from oneself or from the outside, gives satisfaction.[59]

There is a short step between this kind of play or ritual communication to art.

> The child's babbling, of course, does not turn into English or Swahili all by itself. . . . The transition from potential to actual, from genetic inheritance to cultural realization, requires interaction between self and others. This is done mostly through play, invention, and fooling around, in the course of which you notice that the behavior patterns you generate are getting signals in return— "answers" to messages you did not know you had sent. You may then consider, "What did I do to make that happen?"
>
> It is what the drummer does on her drum, what the dancer does in his dance, the lover does in foreplay, what the adventurer does in the great open world: the sending forth of something, and the discovery that it "works." Such probing, sending-out, and playing with the world to see what it will answer, is basic to ritual, to language, and to culture.[60]

According to Driver, the function of ritual is to create or foster order, community, and transformation. For some people, creating, maintaining, and restoring order are, in fact, the most important function of religious ritual. This explains the hostility many people feel toward people dressed as clowns serving communion, women leading worship, or any other innovations that seem to threaten the safety and comfort that they find, for instance, in the pre-Vatican II Mass or the Presbyterian preference for doing things decently and in good order.

Worship

The online version of the Merriam-Webster dictionary defines worship as "the reverence offered a divine being or supernatural power," as well as "an act of expressing such reverence"; "a form of religious practice with its creed and ritual"; and "extravagant respect or admiration for or devotion to an object of esteem." While these notions form the core of what is meant when someone uses the word "worship," they do not address the specific

59. Driver, *Liberating Rites*, 28.
60. Driver, *Liberating Rites*, 29.

activities that Christians might be thinking of when they refer to worship in their church.

At its root, the word "worship" means something like worthiness, that is, the acknowledgment of worth. For many Christians, it tends to mean something like "acknowledging that God is worthy," or, more simply, praising God. However, etymology is only one place to start the discussion of meaning. Another is to note the variety of ways that the word is used in contemporary speech and writing.

Sometimes worship means a relatively brief time of prayer and reflection at the beginning of a meal, meeting, or other gathering which is primarily intended for some other purpose. While this time is more often referred to as "devotions," this usage of "worship" is frequent enough that it bears noting.

More generally in the Christian tradition, worship is the entirety of what happens when the congregation gathers, typically on Sunday mornings, but also at various other times. Worship in this sense means everything from the initial piece of music that is heard as congregants gather (sometimes called the prelude) to the closing hymn, blessing, and dismissal. Worship, in these traditions, includes prayers and responsive readings, hearing scripture read aloud, the sermon or homily, ritual activities such as baptism and communion (which may also be called the Lord's Supper or Eucharist, depending on the denominational or local tradition), as well as hymns and other music. In this book, generally speaking, this is the definition I have in mind when referring to worship.

For others, however, worship means only the initial musical portion of what happens when the congregation gathers. This activity, often lasting a half an hour or more, is usually led by an amplified musical ensemble variously known as the praise team, praise band, or worship leaders. The musicians generally include one or more singers, usually accompanied by some combination of guitars, drums, and electric keyboards. As the musicians perform, the words to the songs (often contemporary praise choruses but sometimes also more traditional hymns) are projected on one or more screens and members of the congregation are encouraged to sing—often swaying with hands upraised—as the songs follow one another without a break. The rest of the service, including the sermon, prayers, and any ritual activity, while certainly worshipful in the sense of being reverent toward God, is not included in this understanding of "worship."

Undefined Lines

This chapter has been an attempt to draw out some of the typical meanings of various words associated with worship, sometimes making careful distinctions and sometimes pointing out the overlaps and similarities. While both art and entertainment have been discussed, only passing mention has been made of how the line between art and entertainment is often one of class and money, in which the pastimes of the elite are considered art, while those of the less wealthy or uneducated are considered entertainment. Thus, the movies are entertainment, while a play is considered art. A rap concert is entertainment, while the symphony orchestra is art. A situation comedy is entertainment, while a PBS documentary is, if not exactly art, at least uplifting.

Looked at another way, while both entertainment and art can cost a lot to produce, generally speaking the monetary rewards are greater for those things that are classed as entertainment than for those that are classed as art. Major movie studios make huge profits, while opera companies and playhouses scramble for donations and grants. Pop stars earn millions, while even highly successful folk singers can barely pay their expenses. Meanwhile, play is for children, unless it is professional sports, which brings things back to issues of money and class.

The line between entertainment and art is sometimes drawn in discussions about the place of the arts in Christian worship, but in many ways entertainment and art are more similar than different. One way to look at the distinctions between the arts, entertainment, and Christian worship is to ask the questions, Who is it for? Who benefits? Who performs? Who is watching, and why?

Some might say that both art and entertainment are for the ego gratification of those who are on stage. All eyes and ears are fixed on them. Even if the production is a flop, there is something very powerful in inhabiting a character other than one's own self or playing an instrument or singing or dancing to the best of one's ability in the presence of an audience. Though relatively few are rewarded by the enormous fame and fortune that come to some, most performers do anticipate and hope for an enormous rush of positive emotion as they receive the applause and adulation of at least their friends and family.

On the other hand, it is equally possible and probably more correct to say that both art and entertainment are for the audience. People come to a play or a concert or a movie to sit in a darkened room where other people (or, in the case of a movie, their photographed images) perform music or pretend to be characters other than themselves, often with remarkable skill. The audience, the listeners, have no part to play other than to become absorbed in what is happening on stage, to allow their emotions and thoughts to be guided by what they see and hear, and to applaud at the end. While being present to such an event may only be a way to pleasurably pass the time, frequently enough audience members come away from a performance with a sense of transcendence, feeling that they have been in the presence of something greater than themselves, or even that they have been irrevocably changed or inspired by what they have seen and heard.

Meanwhile, Christian worship may equally be said to be for the benefit of the worshippers or for the benefit of God. Kierkegaard famously said that in worship, the congregation and the ministers are all performers, and God is the audience. Yet, looked at another way, God, as the source and end of everything, has nothing to gain from human worship. Therefore, worship—like entertainment and art—may be for the people, who in this case come to be changed, inspired, and nourished in order to be the Body of Christ in the world. Or perhaps it is not necessary to ask who it is for, since in the best of art, entertainment, and worship, audiences and congregations, performers and ministers, all participate together with God in an event that connects everyone in a profound communion.

This effort to define the boundaries between art, drama, entertainment, excellence, liturgy, play, prayer, production values, ritual, and worship has, instead, revealed a great deal of overlap and ambiguity. While it seems intuitively correct that they are all related, it is not always clear how connections are made or where one leaves off and another one starts. Rather than giving unambiguous directions, the signposts point down twisting paths that cross and meet in unexpected places. Some of those paths lead to performance and the anxieties that it raises. The next chapter will explore the borders and byways of performance.

five

Performance Anxiety

A high school stage play is more polished than this service we have been rehearsing since the year one. In two thousand years, we have not worked out the kinks. We positively glorify them. Week after week we witness the same miracle: that God is so mighty he can stifle his own laughter. Week after week, we witness the same miracle: that God, for reasons unfathomable, refrains from blowing our dancing bear act to smithereens. Week after week Christ washes the disciples' dirty feet, handles their very toes, and repeats, It is all right—believe it or not—to be people. Who can believe it?[1]

THE NOTIONS OF ENTERTAINMENT and performance are deeply intertwined in Western culture, and thus in the church. In ordinary speech, performers are people who entertain us, whether they sing, dance, act, tell stories, juggle, or play a musical instrument. When we speak of the entertainment industry, we usually mean things like movies, television, popular music, or Broadway musicals. And while the entertainment industry is a major economic and social force in most developed countries, entertainment itself is often dismissed with pejorative words like "useless," "frivolous," "decadent," or the withering adjective "mere."

1. Dillard, "Expedition to the Pole," 38.

As noted at the end of the previous chapter, however, some of the same activities that are disdained as merely entertaining may be seen in a more positive light when described in different ways. What is the difference between a "film" and a movie? What is the difference between a concert at Carnegie Hall and one in a basketball stadium? What is the difference between a Shakespeare play and *Wicked*? What makes the difference between mere entertainment and the uplifting, serious, and culturally important performing arts? Why do we call theatrical productions like *Jesus Christ Superstar* a mere entertainment, while singalong performances of Handel's *Messiah* are treated with utmost reverence?

However these questions are answered, what links all of these activities together is that they depend on performance. Christian worship also depends upon performance, but anxieties arise about "performance" when it is equated with "entertainment." The problem, as Tom Driver explains, is that

> the verb "to perform," like its shorter but not simpler cousin, "to act," is two-faced. On the one side, these words mean "to do," while on the other, they mean "to pretend." This ambiguity tells us much about the kind of actors human beings are.[2]

Driver notes that words like "acting" or "enacting" have been suggested to replace "performing," but they have their own pitfalls:

> If a child is drowning, a person may act to save it. But to act the rescuer is not necessarily to save anyone. I may perform the act of saving the child, and the child will be saved, but I may also perform the same act and no child will be saved because I did it only for the movie camera.[3]

Looking at an action from the other side, he notices a similar ambiguity in the word "observe":

> To observe is to see, as in, "I observe the child playing"; yet to observe is also a certain kind of enactment, as in, "I observe the law," or "At our house we observe the sabbath." Whereas an observation is something seen, an observance is something marked by a special kind of attention or faithfulness, and it has the connotation of something performed at the proper time and in the right way.[4]

2. Driver, *Liberating Rites*, 80.
3. Driver, *Liberating Rites*, 80.
4. Driver, *Liberating Rites*, 81.

It is the ambiguities surrounding the definition of "performance" that has given it a pejorative sense in the church. People become anxious about the connection between performance and entertainment. They ask, what is the difference between doing something well and doing it for show? What is the difference between acting religious and genuine piety? What is the difference between hypocrisy and human fallibility? Some of the answers to these and similar questions may be found in the double meaning of the word "performance," which evokes falsity, a lie, or an avoidance of a deeper truth, on the one hand, and getting things done, on the other.

This chapter examines the problem of performance in Christian worship through the difference between lies, stories, and what is understood as true; the relationship between experience and belief; and the importance and the limits of sincerity and authenticity. It suggests a new understanding of performance that encompasses both the seriousness of ritual and the playfulness of entertainment.

The Problem of Performance

Say the word "performance" in many church circles, and you are bound to get a reaction. Singers and liturgical dancers are quick to explain that what they do in the course of a church service is not a performance, but rather prayer. Declaring that a preacher has been putting on a performance is understood as a cruel insult, carrying overtones of hypocrisy at the very least or even intentionally sinister motives. On the other hand, some people will point out that performance is not a dirty word, that to perform simply means to carry out, accomplish, or fulfill a task.

Part of the problem with the notion of performance is that, as Søren Kierkegaard noted, too many people come to church with the expectation that it is the various ministers who perform the worship, and the congregation's only role is to watch and listen, just as they do in the theater. As in the theater, they may be profoundly moved, but also as in the theater, ultimately they understand themselves as merely an audience, both arriving and leaving as individuals, rather than as members of a congregation who gather as a local expression of the Body of Christ.[5]

By the middle of the twentieth century, this congregational passivity and individuality had become such a problem in the Roman Catholic Church that the Second Vatican Council addressed it directly in its

5. Kierkegaard, *Purity of Heart*, 180–81.

document *Sacrosanctum Concilium*, promulgated by Pope Paul VI in 1963. The authors argued that "fully conscious, and active participation in liturgical celebrations [are] demanded by the very nature of the liturgy"[6] and that it is the duty of the ministers to help the congregation achieve this state. As the conversation about liturgical renewal spread among the Protestant churches, the notion of full, conscious, active participation became an important marker of good worship, with the caveat that listening to a sermon or a choir anthem may be just as fully conscious and active as singing a congregational hymn.

While full, conscious, active participation by every person present is a worthy goal, the reality is that not everyone who comes is equally ready to participate in this way. Some arrive exhausted by their everyday life, wanting nothing more than to sit quietly as the prayers and music wash over them, offering them respite and hope if only for an hour. They want the beauty of the choir's singing to transport them to heaven, and long for the power of the preacher's voice to offer them nothing more than absolution and comfort. As the fourteenth-century preacher mentioned in chapter 3 who lamented that "many folk . . . come only to hear curiosities and new things. Some come only to be seen. Some come only according to the custom and not for devotion nor for their soul's well-being,"[7] many people today come to church for the social engagement, the opportunity to greet their friends during the coffee hour, to see and be seen as an integral part of a community that gathers once a week for mutual support and conversation. Others come out of a sense of duty or obedience, to please an insistent family member or to appease some inner guilt or shame, or simply out of habit. For these, at least, only the people "up front" may be seen as the real participants.

For those who are up front—the preachers, worship leaders, choir directors, and other ministers—there is the ever-present temptation to believe that everyone else has come because of them. When they make their own preaching, singing, or reading scripture into a way to call attention to their own talents and abilities, they no longer perform their duty of inviting the congregation to worship God together. While there is definitely a place for preparation and practice, and even for a certain kind of professional excellence, performance becomes problematic when it becomes the point of the gathering rather than the means through which the congregation offers

6. Second Vatican Council, *Sacrosanctum Concilium*, sec II par 14.

7. Hudson, "Sermons," 223.

its confession and contrition, its prayers of supplication and intercession, its thanksgiving and praise.

Ritual, Authenticity, and Putting On a Show

One of the central issues of the Reformation was the notion of sincerity or authenticity. The reformers accused the Roman Catholic establishment of hypocrisy, of taking bribes in the form of indulgences which promised heaven in exchange for money that lined the pockets of mendacious priests. With the rallying cry of *sola fide*—salvation by faith alone—churches of the Reformation rejected rote prayers and repetitive ritual in favor of genuine repentance and heartfelt conversion to faith in Jesus as one's savior. By the late twentieth century, authenticity—being one's authentic self—had come to be one of the most important values in Western society. As philosopher Peter Kivy says regarding music:

> The highest praise one can bestow nowadays on a musical per-
> formance, in many influential circles, is to say that it was "au-
> thentic." . . . [This word] has become or is close to becoming a
> synonym for "good," while seeming to confer upon a performance
> some magical property that it did not have before. It is the musical
> version of the doctrine of the real presence.[8]

While Kivy is examining the desire of various musicians to reproduce the historically accurate performances of the music of earlier periods, some of what he articulates has some parallels with the desire on the part of certain Christians to reproduce the ethos and/or practice of earlier eras in church history. Just as some musicians may concentrate on plainchant or Palestrina while others specialize in Bach and yet others in Haydn, so some churches may hark back to their particular understanding of the histori-cal Jesus as the only authentic source of Christian teaching, while others look to the pre-Constantinian house-churches, and still others consider the medieval world (either lay or monastic or both) as the authentic Christian-ity which contemporary churches should emulate. Authenticity, in these cases, is derived from the notion of authority, whether that authority is understood to be a particular interpretation of scripture or one or another denominational or historical tradition.

8. Kivy, *Authenticities*, 1.

Kivy examines four possible definitions of the word "authentic." Three of them have to do with historical authenticity, while the fourth is concerned with the personal authenticity of the performer. Kivy's first definition, taken directly from the Oxford English Dictionary, is "possessing original or inherent authority."[9] In music, he says, that would be performing in such a way that the sounds produced are the ones that would have expected to be heard during a composer's lifetime. Musicians who strive for this kind of authenticity play only on instruments that existed at the time the music was composed, sometimes even wearing the clothing appropriate to the period and in settings that approximate the size, shape, and furnishings of rooms for which the music was intended.

The second definition, likewise from the OED, is "original, firsthand, or prototypical,"[10] as opposed to copied. Conceding that this kind of authenticity is difficult to explain when it comes to music, Kivy begins his discussion of this sense of "authentic" with an example from the visual arts: there is only one, original *Night Watch*, and anything else that purports to be it is either a copy or a forgery.

This leads to the third definition, which is "genuine," as opposed to counterfeit or forged. An authentic performance, according to this definition, is one which "follows the intentions, wishes, and instructions with regard to the performance of that work that the composer has made known to us, or that we infer."[11] This goes beyond the merely historical sounds of the first distinction to include the formal and expressive features that the composer indicated in the original score.

The fourth definition of "authentic"—belonging or proper to oneself—moves away from any appeal to historical correctness, to a focus on the musician as a performing artist. In this case, the question is not the desires or intentions of the composer, but rather the interpretation of the composer's ideas and intentions. As Kivy puts it, a performance described as authentic in this sense is

> characterized as autonomous, sincere, self-originating, original, an expression of the performer rather than of someone whom the performer is aping. . . . It is just this kind of authenticity—originality,

---

9. Kivy, *Authenticities*, 3.

10. Kivy, *Authenticities*, 3.

11. Kivy, *Authenticities*, 5.

not slavish imitation; sincerity and truth to oneself, not false consciousness—that we tend to think the artist should have.[12]

While, as noted earlier, many churches strive to ground their authority in certain scriptural texts or certain aspects of tradition, the notion of
authenticity as being true to oneself has come to be seen as a critical virtue
in contemporary life. This, of course, is not a new idea, as the popular motto
"to thine own self be true" comes from a speech given by Polonius in Shakespeare's *Hamlet*. The opposite of being true to oneself, being authentic, is to
be false—a liar, a hypocrite, or simply someone who does what is conventional and expected rather than acting out of inner conviction or genuine
desire. The kind of self-help advice that counsels readers to follow their
heart, regardless of familial or even economic pressure to do something
more sensible or conventional, grows out of this elevation of authenticity
as a primary value.

A synonym for authenticity is "sincerity." In their volume *Ritual and
Its Consequences*, Adam Seligman, Robert Weller, Michael Puett, and Ben-
nett Simon posit sincerity and ritual as opposites:

> Sincerity often grows out of a reaction against ritual. It criticizes
> ritual's acceptance of social convention as mere action (perhaps just
> acting) without intent, as performance without belief. The alterna-
> tives it often suggests are categories that grow out of individual
> soul-searching rather than the acceptance of social conventions.
> Sincerity thus grows out of abstract and generalized categories
> generated within individual consciousness. The sincere mode of
> behavior seeks to replace the "mere convention" of ritual with a
> genuine and thoughtful state of internal conviction. Rather than
> becoming what we do in action through ritual, we do according
> to what we have become through self-examination. This form of
> thought emphasizes tropes of "authenticity," and each individual
> thus takes on an enormous responsibility.[13]

The authors are quick to acknowledge that sincerity has an important place in human interaction. They contrast, for instance, the imper-
sonal handshake that is shared with strangers after a concert in a symphony
hall with the warm, heartfelt handshake offered to a former dear friend
with whom one may no longer have much in common but nonetheless is

12. Kivy, *Authenticities*, 6.
13. Seligman, Weller, Puett, and Simon, *Ritual*, 103.

thought of with warmth and care.[14] They argue, however, that sincerity has limits that are largely overlooked, and that those limits are precisely where ritual is needed:

> Our contemporary period is marked by an overwhelming concern with sincerity at the expense of ritual. This pervasiveness is, to a significant degree, a result of the strong role of Protestant Christianity in the making of our modern world and of contemporary culture (even as this world is shared by Jews, Confucians, Hindus, Muslims, Sikhs, and so on). . . . Ritual has had something of a poor reputation in the contemporary world, relegated to a form of deviance in the structural-functionalism of midcentury American sociology, or extirpated as an empty, external husk, lacking in ultimate spiritual significance, or, again, condemned as a form of authoritarian control and dominance. We are often too concerned with exploring the different forms of self-expression and of individual authenticity to appreciate the rhythmic structure of the shared subjunctive that is the deepest work of ritual.[15]

Ritual, for Seligman and his colleagues, is an important corrective to what they see as the current overvaluing of sincerity, arguing that there is a price to pay for its absence. Ritual, as they and others in the field of ritual studies suggest, is how societies and individuals renegotiate boundaries. Through ritual, people learn to live with one another by creating a temporary order through the construction of a performative, subjunctive world, an "as-if" world in which what is said and done has real effects that last beyond it.[16]

Sincerity's charge against ritual is that ritual is just putting on a show. There is something dismissive in this common phrase, beginning with the word "just," which asserts that what comes next is something of no value. To put on a show in this sense is to do something that at best is worthless, and at worst intentionally deceitful. However, at its most basic meaning, to put on a show is to prepare a performance of some kind—a play, a concert, a ballet, or an evening of vaudeville—for the entertainment or pleasure or even the edification of an audience.

In the classic novel *Little Women*, Jo March and her sisters amuse themselves and their mother by putting on a play for their friends as part of

14. Seligman, Weller, Puett, and Simon, *Ritual*, 5.
15. Seligman, Weller, Puett, and Simon, *Ritual*, 10.
16. Seligman, Weller, Puett, and Simon, *Ritual*, 11.

their Christmas celebration. This innocent pastime helps the family endure the hardships of winter in New England without the comfort and support of the girls' father, who is away serving as a chaplain during the Civil War. Although the play itself has no religious content, and indeed is an over-wrought romance written by the teenaged Jo, there is no intimation that this kind of putting on a show is deceitful, immoral, or otherwise problematic, even at Christmas in the home of a clergyman. While the event in *Little Women* is relatively elaborate for a children's production, many children even today, like Jo and her sisters, enjoy organizing more or less impromptu shows, inviting their parents and anyone else who might be willing to watch and applaud as they sing or dance or act out stories.

Despite the popularity of both adults and children participating in amateur theatrics, as well as the wide acclaim of professional efforts in the performing arts, to "put on a show" or "put on an act" has come to mean being false, deceptive, or otherwise dishonest. Sometimes this is done for benign reasons, such as when parents put on a show of being strong or upbeat in order to care for their children in the face of tragedy, or when a teacher who has heard bad news during recess nonetheless carries on with the scheduled lecture or class discussion. At other times, however, to put on a show means to be pretentious, to act as if one is better than others, to make something out of nothing, or to pretend to like someone who is present while speaking ill of them behind their back. Those who habitually indulge in pretenses like these are considered inauthentic or insincere and are often shunned or at least laughed at behind *their* backs.

Unlike either amateur theatrics or putting on a pretentious show, authentic ritual is the practice of beneficial forms of behavior that do not necessarily come naturally. Just as children learn to say "please" and "thank you" ritualistically even when they do not yet feel grateful, the regular practice of the ritual of communion teaches Christians to honor all eating and drinking as a gift from God. Kneeling at another person's feet and having one own's feet ritually washed on Maundy Thursday can help participants learn something important about both offering and accepting service. Regularly offering signs of peace to one's neighbor during worship can become an unintentional moment of healing and reconciliation, as each has the opportunity to unexpectedly see Christ in the face of the other.

Lies, Made-Up Stories, and Telling the Truth

"What is truth?" Pontius Pilate asked Jesus, questioning his claim that "everyone who belongs to the truth listens to my voice."[17] Philosophers and theologians argue about the precise definition of truth and how we know what is true, using words like "alethiology" and "epistemology" to describe such fields of study. Picasso is famously said to have made the observation that art is a lie that tells the truth. But what is a lie? How do we know what is true? What kind of truths can be told through the arts? What is the difference between facts and truth? And what does all that imply for what we do when we gather together on Sunday mornings?

Long before the birth of Jesus, philosophers noted the difference between fiction and reality. In *Performing the Sacred: Theology and Theater in Dialogue*, Dale Savidge writes:

> Aristotle, in his *Poetics*, first sets poetry (and the mimetic arts in general) apart from philosophy, education, and politics by stating that the purpose of poetry is aesthetic. Art brings pleasure, first and only; if it teaches, that is incidental to its character. Our English word "pleasure" is perhaps too debased now to adequately convey the elevated nature of this response. Aristotle does not dismiss the moral content of art because morality is a necessary contributor to the aesthetic experience. His point is that artists are not to pursue education, moral or otherwise, but rather to create out of their own ethical and moral sensibility a work of art that brings pleasure to the reader/audience. This pleasure involves *catharsis*, or a purgation of unhealthy emotions (pity and fear) through the audiences' vicarious experience of the suffering of the tragic hero. It is in the pleasurable experience that the audience is instructed, matured, and prodded.[18]

Part of that pleasurable experience, or what Savidge and others refer to as the aesthetic, is that poetry, music, dance, and other arts are not the same thing as everyday experience. Even when a drama portrays a story based in facts, all but the most pedantic recognize that sometimes the facts need to be altered to create a better story. Sometimes the chronology is changed, sometimes a character is added or subtracted, sometimes words that the playwright could never have known about are put into someone's mouth. It is not the facts themselves, but rather how they are portrayed that

17. John 18:37–38.
18. Johnson and Savidge, *Performing*, 33–34.

move us. Part of the pleasure in a novel, a movie, or a play is the suspension of disbelief, the willingness to enter into the constructed world as if it were true, even though it is obvious that it is not.

When parents and teachers tell children not to lie, it is pretty clear that the point is to not intentionally deceive anyone. Those same parents and teachers, though, probably read the children books about elves and monsters and animals that talk like humans, take them to the movies, or make up stories about what their stuffed animals are thinking as they converse in pretend animal voices. Most children play at being police officers or cooks or mommies and daddies, wear princess or pirate costumes on Halloween, or act out scenes from the Bible in which they are King David or Ruth or Mary or even Jesus. Eventually, most children figure out that there is a difference between a lie and a made-up story, between deception and make-believe. They learn that a lie is a deliberate attempt to deceive, to make someone believe what they themselves know is not true. A made-up story, on the other hand, requires that both they and their listeners agree from the outset that what is being said is not objectively true. Most children learn that it can be delightful, instructive, or even transformative to pretend to be someone else in a movie or a play or a game, but that pretending to be who they are not in their everyday life usually comes with serious negative consequences.

When Picasso spoke about art as a lie that tells the truth, he was not simply being provocative. Just as a painting, no matter how convincing it seems, is not the same thing as the view from a window, so a play is not the same thing as real life, and watching a movie is not the same thing as being in the presence of the actors. Although it may contain many facts, a novel does not present a factual account of something that happened in ordinary life. Nonetheless, all of these art forms are capable of revealing something true and important about the human condition, about the world at large, or even about God. There is no intent to deceive. When Jesus told a parable, he did not claim that the story he was telling had actually happened to any particular person. Nevertheless, it is clear that his hearers understood that a deep truth was being revealed. A story does not have to be factual to have the ring of truth, to convey something true about what it means to be human, to portray a vision of what life was like in the past or might be in the future, or to suggest new understandings about inner motivations and outward actions.

Novels, plays, and the parables of Jesus are made-up stories. A lie, on the other hand, is an intentional attempt to deceive, to make someone else believe something that the speaker knows to be untrue. While certain lies are considered at least marginally acceptable if they are said to keep from doing greater harm, most lies are destructive to the kind of trust that fosters human flourishing. To call someone a liar in private is to utter a serious insult; to call someone a liar in public is to invite a lawsuit for defamation of character, if not a physical fight. Lies invite suspicion, causing pain and confusion among those who find out that they have acted upon false information.

Truth, as Pontius Pilate famously implied, can be defined in many ways. At one level, telling the truth means sticking to objectively observable facts. However, one can hide the truth by using facts selectively, obscure it with explanations that are plausible, or embroider it with extraneous details. While some people hold that some things are absolutely true, always and everywhere, others hold that truth is relative, with facts or circumstances that are obvious and incontrovertible to one person being invisible or irrelevant to another. Still others acknowledge that while there may, indeed, be some truths that are absolute, it is not possible for humans to know them with certainty due to the inevitable bias each person brings to every situation.

Whatever one believes about absolute truth, there are certain truths that most human societies agree upon. "It is better to tell the truth than to lie" is one of them. Another is that the truth of the human condition is better known through the arts—through stories, poetry, and song—than through more discursive means. Whatever one believes about the absolute, historical truth of scripture, the stories that have been handed down for centuries and continue to be told and retold in the assembly on Sunday mornings help Christians learn who they are as the Body of Christ.

Symbols of Belief

Belief is not the same thing as either knowledge or truth. People of good will can differ about their beliefs without being accused of lying. Nevertheless, people tend to believe that what they see, hear, and feel in their own bodies is true. Physical experiences are often given symbolic or metaphoric significance, as is evidenced in such common English expressions as "seeing is believing" or "I see what you mean." In his discussion of the fourth century baptismal homilies of Cyril of Jerusalem, Ambrose, John Chrysostom, and Theodore of Mopsuestia, Edward Yarnold asserts that these sermons "take us back to an enviable age when people were so sensitive to symbols that the liturgy could be left to speak for itself."[19] While it is arguable whether people were more sensitive to symbols in earlier ages than they are today, or that the liturgy was ever left to speak for itself without commentary and explanation, it is certainly true that today many people both inside and outside the church tend to devalue symbolic representation. It is not unusual for someone to say, "Oh, that is *only* a symbol" or "It is *just* a symbolic gesture," as if symbols had no ability to affect human understanding. To devalue symbols, and the ritual events with which they are intimately tied, is characteristic of post-Enlightenment patterns of thought in which only that which can be measured, counted, or otherwise quantified is understood to be real.

To refer to something as *merely* symbolic is to imply that it has no substance or reality. However, every human culture is made up of symbolic systems. A symbol is something that means something other than what it objectively is. What people wear, how they style their hair, whether they carry a briefcase or a handbag, and many other conscious and unconscious decisions are not simply matters of practicality, but rather are symbols conveying something about their social role. Symbols such as uniforms, tattoos, hats, and other forms of adornment have real effects in how people treat one another. Flags, as symbols of political entities, evoke real feelings of patriotism or enmity or fear. Logos, typefaces, and even colors which may symbolize such mundane products as washing detergent or yogurt have real effects on what people buy and use. Money, whether embodied in gold, physical dollar bills, or electronic bits of information, is a symbol of what kinds of work and objects are more valued than others. Language itself is a symbol system in which mostly arbitrary sounds refer to objects, relationships, events, and concepts in increasingly complex and sophisticated ways. To a very large extent, beyond the basic animal needs such as air, food, water, rest, and companionship, symbols are the reality that define most people's lives.

Not all symbols are completely arbitrary, however. While it would be hard for someone who had no knowledge of the complex customs surrounding marriage in the Western world to guess the meaning of a wedding ring, everyone knows how food, water, and fire, for instance, can almost

19. Yarnold, *Awe-Inspiring Rites*, ix.

instantly convey symbolic levels of meaning. Regardless of any individual's consciousness awareness or intellectual ideas, symbols that are deeply rooted in common human experience have the power to touch them deeply. In his discussion of the mystagogic sermons heard by the newly baptized in the second half of the fourth century, which chapter 3 examines in some detail, Yarnold says the preacher would

> explain the sacraments of baptism, confirmation, and Holy Communion by which a Christian became a full member of the Church. The ceremonies took place at night, some of them in the dark, after weeks of intense preparation; they were wrapped in secrecy and the candidate knew little about them until just before, or even after, [they] had received them. Everything was calculated to inspire religious awe, to make these rites the occasion of a profound and life-long conversion.[20]

Things like fasting, food, sweetness, darkness, surprise, and other elements of early Christian initiation rites can have equally powerful effects on modern persons regardless of their conscious, intellectual ideas about symbols. However, as the mystagogic sermons illustrate, even when symbols connect to primal experiences of hunger, thirst, fear, or similar physical/emotional states, it is still necessary to teach participants what those symbols mean in a particular context. While such symbols connect to universal human experiences, each can have different specific meanings to different persons or groups. Although everyone shares the primal experience of hunger, each person or group attaches different stories and interpretations to eating after a long fast. It is these stories and interpretations that the mystagogic sermons were meant to teach the new Christians.

In the Reformation and the Age of Enlightenment that followed, the explanations came to have more importance than the actual symbols. Since that time, it has become clear to at least some people that whether one is raising children, selling soap, or preaching the Gospel, explanation alone is often insufficient. Others seem not to agree, especially when it comes to matters of faith, preferring preaching that appeals more to reason than to the emotions. In her discussion of various approaches to preaching, homiletician Jana Childers notes:

> Through the beginning of the twentieth century, persuasive appeals in their many and various forms (rational, emotional, or volitional) were a major force in preaching. . . . Although mid-century

20. Yarnold, *Awe-Inspiring Rites*, ix.

neo-orthodoxy refocused preachers' attention on encounter models and later-century transformational approaches have shifted the homiletical agenda once again, the long reign of the persuasion model is far from over. Even at the end of the twentieth century, many preachers still preach as if listeners could be argued into the realm of God.[21]

Childers is making a case for new approaches to preaching rather than addressing other elements of worship, but her larger point is that worship is an event to be encountered with more than the intellect. She and others have rediscovered what the ancient church had always known: deep, elemental symbols speak to the whole person, opening them up to the presence of God.

Pretending as Practice

Much of children's play is a kind of practice for what they will do when they are grown up. They pretend to be firefighters or police officers or teachers or nurses or rap singers or football players because those are activities that they see adults doing, and the children want to do them too. They pretend to be princesses or knights in shining armor or famous athletes or characters from whatever movie they have recently seen because they want to be like their heroes. They talk to their dolls as if they were real, live babies. They make cookies and cakes out of mud as if it were real food. They know—or learn quickly —that they cannot really eat the mud and that the dolls do not respond of their own volition, but while they are engaged in the game, they behave as if what they are pretending is real.

This as-if quality that is inherent in play extends to many other kinds of interactions in everyday life. As Adam Seligman and his colleagues point out, saying please and thank you, for instance, creates an illusion of equality that may not actually exist:

> When we ask our children to please clear their plates or our students to please open their books, declining is not a normal option. Nevertheless, we act *as if* [emphasis in original] the behavior were voluntary because that ritual creates the social world that allows our interactions to continue in peace. Rituals such as saying "please" and "thank you" create an illusion, but with no attempt to deceive. This is a crucial difference from a lie, which is an

21. Childers, *Performing the Word*, 34.

illusion with a clear attempt to deceive the other. In this ritual is much more like play, which is the joint entrance into an illusionary world.[22]

Every society has its own set of customs and rituals, its own etiquette, that sets up joint illusions in which individuals come to understand what is expected of them in whatever role they find themselves. As children learn these rituals, they enter ever more proficiently into the socially constructed as-if world in which they will live as adults. They also come to realize that their daily experience is not always identical to that subjunctive, as-if world.

Describing the common experience of a parent reading a bedtime story to a young child and the way they go about choosing what to read, how to read it, discussing whether the giant *really* threatened to eat Jack, and deciding who gets to recite each part in what voices and with what gestures, Seligman and his colleagues argue that such repetitive rituals help to form the personal identities of those who participate as well as the relationships between them. They write,

> The enactment and the negotiation require from both child and parent a capacity to relax and re-form boundaries; to shuttle back and forth between "is it really true" and "pretend"; to shuffle roles and expectations; to imagine past, present, and future; and somehow to conclude, knowing all this will be repeated countless more times. In principle, what will allow variations and ultimately the evolution of new rituals is that the repetitions are building up certain structures inside the child, and that the [parent-child] pair can move into a different orbit, as it were, in working on new sets of issues requiring imagination and repetition.[23]

Similarly, the authors suggest, regular participation in communal Christian worship may be understood as a repeated immersion in a subjunctive, as-if activity, an identity- and faith-forming practice in which one may not initially or always believe every word of the Creed that is recited every Sunday, sincerely love each person in the room, nor think that prayer makes any difference in the world. However, by saying or singing the words week after week, by offering a blessing to whoever is nearby when it is time to pass the peace, by confessing and giving thanks and praying for all the broken places in the world as if they were sincere, participants may come

22. Seligman, Weller, Puett, and Simon, *Ritual,* 21–22.
23. Seligman, Weller, Puett, and Simon, *Ritual,* 48.

to believe in the nearness of God, to behave toward others in more loving ways, to take on the habit of daily prayer and meditation.

This "fake it till you make it" attitude is at odds with the commonly held values of sincerity and authenticity in many faith communities as well as in much of society at large, at least in North America. Young people especially are prone to hurl accusations of hypocrisy, rather than fallibility, at adults who do not live up to their professed ideals in every instance. Even so, there are limits to what sincerity makes possible, and it is at these limits that ritual becomes necessary. Since even sincere believers regularly fall short of their Christian ideals, the regular practice of ritual serves to strengthen their ability to perceive the already-present realm of God, even though it is theologically understood as not yet fully realized.

Preaching as Performance

Cleophus LaRue teaches preaching at Princeton Theological Seminary, but the style of preaching that he discusses in his book *I Believe I'll Testify* is far from the unadorned plain style of the Reformed tradition commonly associated with that institution.[24] Like others cited elsewhere in this volume, LaRue notes the growing changes in Christian worship with regard to style, form of expression, and ways of talking about and to God. He discusses the differences not only between White and Black preaching, but the tension between those who favor and those who would oppose reforming worship in the direction of gender-inclusive and nonmilitaristic language; those who prefer the praise choruses that others disparage as "7-11" songs (seven words sung eleven times) and those who adhere to the old hymns as the only proper music for the church; those for whom Father, Son, and Holy Spirit are either the only proper names for God or conventions to be avoided.

LaRue understands preaching, especially in the African American style, as performance. His discussion of the uses of imagination in preparing a sermon include techniques that seem very similar to those an actor would use in preparing for a new role:

> Initial imaginative thoughts are probably the closest things to the madness and sensual thoughts about which the early writers warned us. These are the first thoughts that come flowing from our innermost being. Sometimes these ideas flow from our lived

24. La Rue, *Believe I'll Testify*, 71.

experience before we even read a passage of Scripture. At such times it is experience in search of Scripture. At other times ideas flow when we reflect momentarily on a biblical passage as we remember it. Still at other times it is a fresh reading of and/or a sustained focus on Scripture that stirs the imagination. Something in experience or in Scripture pricks the imagination, and the flow begins in earnest.[25]

Simply substitute "the script" where LaRue says "scripture" to see the similarity.

In tracing the roots of what many people think of as the typical style of Black preachers today, LaRue describes the artful language of the frequently illiterate folk preachers who ministered to enslaved persons on pre-Civil War plantations. Noting that White evangelical preachers used similar oratorical techniques, he describes the folk sermon as

a formulaic structure based on phrases, verses, and whole passages the preacher knew by heart. Characterized by repetition, parallelisms, dramatic use of voice and gesture, and a whole range of oratorical devices, the sermon began with normal conversational prose, then built to a rhythmic cadence, regularly marked by exclamations of the congregation, and climaxes in a tonal change accompanied by shouting, singing, and ecstatic behavior.[26]

This pattern is often seen in African-American churches still today, as many Black preachers continue to prefer to enter the pulpit with only a mental outline, rather than a fully written text. Even those who do begin with a carefully crafted, written sermon, LaRue says, "more often than not spontaneously translate it into sermonese in the pulpit."[27] This appearance of spontaneity, LaRue points out, is important in congregations that value the dynamic pattern of call and response between preacher and people, noting that "unless the Spirit roused the congregation to move and shout, the sermon was essentially unsuccessful."[28] Preachers in this tradition want to claim divine inspiration, "for it is that claim that gives them their authority in the pulpit. Their authority comes when the congregation believes preachers are channeling God or that God is speaking through them."[29]

25. La Rue, *Believe I'll Testify*, 75–76.
26. La Rue, *Believe I'll Testify*, 84.
27. La Rue, *Believe I'll Testify*, 85.
28. La Rue, *Believe I'll Testify*, 84.
29. La Rue, *Believe I'll Testify*, 87.

LaRue has ancient precedent for his understanding of preaching as performance. In *The Preacher as Liturgical Artist,* Trygve Johnson considers the traditional roles of the preacher as teacher and herald, arguing that the contemporary situation calls for an additional role of the preacher as a liturgical artist. Appealing to historical precedent, he shows that Augustine of Hippo was an early proponent of preachers understanding themselves primarily as teachers, by which he meant, among other things, practitioners of the art of rhetoric in which he himself had been trained. In Augustine's time, rhetoric was suspect among Christians because it was a tool used by pagan orators to persuade people to embrace various pagan philosophies:

> The early Christian church, forced to carve out an identity in a world saturated in the eloquence of pagan wisdom, sometimes viewed anything that represented secular culture as a threat to the identity and practice of the church. One could say that "worldly" association tainted rhetoric of many Christians and inspired them to fortify themselves against any form of engagement with such "worldly" matters.[30]

While the use of the term "secular" to describe the culture of late antiquity is somewhat anachronistic, the point that Johnson wants to make is that rhetoric was viewed as not neutral but rather as integrally related to the values and mores of pagan culture. As Christianity became a state religion under Constantine, preachers like Augustine and his contemporary, John Chrysostom, began to think of rhetoric more pragmatically, adapting it to the new situation. Johnson continues, "As Christian preachers began to take public ownership for conditions in society after years of social marginalization and even persecution, they began to learn the fine arts of classical antiquity with great effectiveness."[31] In book 4 of *On Christian Doctrine,* Augustine argues:

> Now, the art of rhetoric being available for the enforcing either of truth or falsehood, who will dare to say that truth in the person of its defenders is to take its stand unarmed against falsehood? For example, that those who are trying to persuade men of what is false are to know how to introduce their subject, so as to put the hearer into a friendly, or attentive, or teachable frame of mind, while the defenders of the truth shall be ignorant of that art? That the former are to tell their falsehoods briefly, clearly, and plausibly,

30. Johnson, *Preacher as Liturgical Artist,* 56.
31. Johnson, *Preacher as Liturgical Artist,* 57.

while the latter shall tell the truth in such a way that it is tedious to listen to, hard to understand, and, in fine, not easy to believe it? That the former are to oppose the truth and defend falsehood with sophistical arguments, while the latter shall be unable either to defend what it true, or to refute what is false? That the former, while imbuing the minds of their hearers with erroneous opinions, are by their power of speech to awe, to melt, to enliven, and to rouse them, while the latter shall in defence of the truth be sluggish, and frigid, and somnolent? Who is such a fool as to think this wisdom? Since, then, the faculty of eloquence is available for both sides, and is of very great service in the enforcing either of wrong or right, why do not good men study to engage it on the side of truth, when bad men use it to obtain the triumph of wicked and worthless causes, and to further injustice and error?[32]

Johnson says that Augustine is able to put rhetoric to Christian ends "not because of his status and authority as a secular rhetorician, nor because he is a trusted bishop, but because he honestly does not see a problem in doing so."[33] Similar arguments could be made for the use of video, praise bands, and other elements of contemporary entertainment in worship today. Augustine's reminder that a teacher "must speak so as to teach, to delight, and to persuade"[34] echoes down the centuries, giving liberty to those whose style of worship or preaching others dismiss as mere entertainment.

Pilgrimage, Procession, and Dancing in the Aisles

LaRue makes the point that worship is always changing, and that much that is taken for granted today was widely contested in earlier eras. For example, he says, "in the nineteenth century some in the African Methodist Episcopal Church did not approve of organs and choirs, considering them to be the work of the devil." Similarly, Bishop Daniel Alexander Payne, an important shaper of the AME church, believed that an educated clergy should dress in plain clothing rather than robes, and "favored a strict adherence to the worship service outlined in the AME discipline and was, therefore, opposed to dance, song and spirit possession."[35]

32. Augustine, *On Christian Doctrine*, 4.2.3.

33. Johnson, *Preacher as Liturgical Artist*, 59.

34. Augustine, *On Christian Doctrine*, 4.12.27

35. LaRue, *Believe I'll Testify*, 40.

While LaRue is writing about the African American experience, similar views were and continue to be widespread in other communities as well. Not everyone agrees, however. While quiet and decorum are still highly prized in some denominations and local churches, others encourage a more physically ecstatic form of congregational participation.

Recently a friend related a story about a long-ago pastor at a Roman Catholic church who would enter the sanctuary dancing to begin Sunday worship. The friend remembered:

> He didn't do this every week, but often enough that it was not an unusual sight. He loved bright vestments, and his dance was a merry, twirling affair, generally to a lively musical accompaniment. There were those in the parish who never quite got used to it or considered it priestly. Many others, definitely including me, wanted to dance too! This man, in both his words and his actions, made it clear to us that worshipping God was an occasion for joy and enthusiasm, lifting voices, feet, and hearts to praise Creation.[36]

As Aiden Cavanaugh pointedly reminds his readers, movement and procession are an integral part of the common liturgical inheritance of the church. In many churches, worship begins with a procession or entrance rite. Some processions are very formal and stylized, with white-clad acolytes carrying a cross, candles, and perhaps a festal banner leading robed choir members and clergy through the center of the nave toward the altar. At the offertory later in the service, members of the congregation wearing their ordinary clothing may solemnly bring the bread and cup forward from the back of the church to be blessed for communion. At other times, the entire congregation might move from their seats in the nave to surround the font in order to participate in a baptism. On Good Friday, everyone might gather in the streets to process through the neighborhood surrounding the church as they carry statues of Jesus and Mary, sing hymns, and act out moments of Christ's final walk through Jerusalem on the day of his crucifixion.

The Good Friday processions that are so much a part of Latin Catholic culture are in many ways a particularly elaborate version of the Stations of the Cross devotion, which has been a staple of Roman Catholic devotional life since about the fourteenth century. This practice has its origins much earlier. At least as early as the fourth century, pilgrims went to Jerusalem desiring to walk in the footsteps of Jesus along what is still known today as the Via Dolorosa, the Road of Sorrows. The account of one such traveler,

36. John Morris, letter to author, 2018.

known as Egeria, is discussed in chapter 3. As travel from Western Europe to Jerusalem became increasingly difficult during the periods when that city was held by various Muslim rulers in the twelfth through the fourteenth centuries, devout Christians began to designate certain places along the walls of their local church or in the churchyard as physical commemorations of Christ's passion. Eventually, these places came to include statues or images depicting particular moments in Christ's journey to the cross. Although the number of the stations has varied at different times and places, the devotion became formalized with fourteen stations at which the faithful pause and reflect on the meaning of each moment and recite appropriate, prescribed prayers. In this way, what had begun as a pilgrimage became a procession, especially when groups of the devout gather to pray the stations together during Lent or at other times.

Liturgical dancers often make the point that any procession is a form of dance. This is especially evident when those who are processing take pains to walk with a careful, measured gait, ensuring that the entire group moves together as one body. One way to do this is to use the step that dancers call the *tripudium* (Latin for "three steps"), which consists of taking three steps forward and one step back.

According to dance historian Donna LaRue, references to the use of the tripudium in both pagan and Christian worship are found in various written sources dating from about 200 BCE to 1600 CE. These references, however, are often confusing and contradictory, and often seem to describe something quite different than the pattern that dancers today call by that name. Indeed, tripudium in the ancient sources can mean either "dance" or "joy." In addition, since the meaning of dance can itself be a metaphor for joy rather than an indicator of actual dancing, LaRue cautions that

> one must be careful not to over-interpret a source as a direct reference to dance merely because it contains the term *tripudium*.
>
> When *tripudium* does mean "dance," the temptation exists to prove that it signifies a specific kind of danced movement. Some scholars associate such varied meanings as "three-step," "hop-dance," "line-" and "circle-dance," and "religious dance" with *tripudium*.[37]

LaRue, however, is not willing to associate any particular movement with the word in ancient times, or even any evidence of liturgical dance in the early church, on the basis of such thin evidence. There is better evidence

37. LaRue, "Tripudium," 26.

for liturgical dance in the Middle Ages. Larue notes that music historian Jacques Chailley has discovered at least two hymns with dance rubrics in the fourteenth century chapterbook of Sens Cathedral, although it is not clear that the word "tripudium" is used in these texts.[38] While the tripudium of today may neither be a direct connection to ancient liturgical dances nor the "merry, twirling affair" of that twentieth-century Catholic priest, there is ample evidence to suggest that dancing in the aisles in church is not simply a recent phenomenon. Even so, for LaRue, it is unnecessary to ground defenses for contemporary liturgical dance in such obscure historical evidence. As she puts it, "the real need is to uphold dance as a gift given to be given, a sacrificial offering of the body at prayer, a eucharistic gift in kind for the gift of life."[39]

Entertainment and Efficacy

The as-if world of performance and pretending is often dismissed in Protestant culture as mere entertainment, a useless waste of time fit only for the hopelessly immature, certainly not edifying and possibly even sinful. In other traditions, the lines between entertainment and worship, between play and utility, are not so clear. The anthropological reflections of ritual studies pioneer Richard Schechner offer some insights into how that may be.

In his essay "From Ritual to Theatre and Back: The Structure/Process of the Efficacy-Entertainment Dyad," Schechner describes a recurrent series of events in the life of the Tsembaga of Highlands, New Guinea. Every twelve to fifteen years, the Tsembaga people declare a festival year, called a *kaiko*, in which instead of conducting war, local groups host one another for a few days of dancing, feasting, and trading various goods. Schechner describes the festivities as "a transformation of combat techniques into entertainment."[40] Movements, sounds, costumes, and other elements that are usually used in battle are transformed into dancing, with everyone dancing with everyone else at some point in the celebration. Feasting is also integral to the event, with great piles of food on display while the dancing

38. LaRue, "Tripudium," 28.
39. LaRue, "Tripudium," 29.
40. Schechner, *Essays*, 64.

is going on. As he puts it, "What starts in dancing ends in eating; or, to put it in artistic-religious terms, what starts as theatre ends as communion."[41]

While entertainment might be understood simply as fun or aesthetic enjoyment, Schechner uses the term in a very specific way, including within it both participatory dancing and the theatrical reenactment that is integral to the social, economic, and spiritual well-being of the community. Noting that there is war among neighboring groups between the *kaiko* years in which there is peace, he writes:

> The exact transformation of combat behavior into performance is at the heart of the *kaiko*. This transformation is identical in structure to that at the heart of Greek theatre (and from the Greeks down throughout all of Western theatre history). Namely, the characterization and the presentation of real or possible events— the story, plot or dramatic action worked out among human figures (whether they be called men or gods)—is a transformation of real behavior into symbolic behavior. In fact, transformation is at the heart of theatre, and there appear to be only two fundamental kinds of theatrical transformation: (1) the displacement of anti-social, injurious, disruptive behavior by ritualized gesture and display and (2) the invention of characters who act out fictional events or real events fictionalized by virtue of their being acted out (as in documentary theatre or Roman gladiatorial games).[42]

The details of such transformations vary from community to community, and, like the manhood initiation of boys in certain Australian or African tribes, they may be understood as integral to the proper functioning of a society. While Schechner discusses such theatricality as entertainment, it is easy to see how the *kaiko* may also be considered as ritual. It is important to remember that ritual, when properly understood, is not empty words and gestures, but rather action and speech that is intended to accomplish some desired end. For this reason, efficacy or utility is not opposed to ritual, as is often assumed in Protestant thought, but identified with it. As Tom Driver puts it:

> Rituals are primarily instruments designed to change a situation. They are more like washing machines than books. A book may be *about* something, but the machine takes in dirty clothes and, if all goes well, transforms them into cleaner ones.[43]

41. Schechner, *Essays*, 66.
42. Schechner, *Essays*, 66.
43. Driver, *Liberating Rites*, 93.

Thus, rituals effect transformations:

> There is no way to become a priest of the church without a rite of
> ordination, and no way to become a member of most churches
> without having undergone baptism. Rites of passage are per-
> formed not simply to *mark* transition but to *affect* them [emphasis
> in original].[44]

Ritual, then, is an important aspect of what happens when a congregation gathers for worship. Indeed, it might be said that the entire event,
from the moment that individuals leave their homes with the intention to
worship together until they scatter to their separate lives at the end of the
benediction is itself a complex ritual. Unlike much contemporary art, ritual
is not about itself or even about the individual self. Rather, to the extent that
it is "about" anything, it is about human relationships to one another and to
the divine. What rituals do, ultimately, is help people remember who they
are in relation to one another and in relation to God.

While the efficacy of ritual does not depend entirely on how it is
performed, artful performance often plays an integral part in helping participants feel that something important has happened. Many of the tools
and skills are similar to those used in theatrical entertainments; however,
they are used for a very different purpose. And, unlike the illusion that is
integral to a play or a movie, what people do and say in worship are actually
done and said, not a pretense even if done in the subjunctive, as-if sense.

Performing, Embodiment, and Showing Off

There are many words and actions that, in the right circumstances, perform
or enact or effect an existential change in one or more persons. Ritual theo-
rists call these words and actions performative. Performative words and
actions matter in a way that is different from ordinary words and actions.
Although they have a ritual quality, they are not necessarily religious in
nature, occurring in many different social and professional situations. For
instance, before the boss said, "You are fired," everyone in the department
worked for the company; now someone is unemployed. Before the person
who is It touches someone else and says, "Tag, you're It," the other person
was one of the crowd; now the new It is obliged to chase rather than be
chased. Before the jury foreperson says, "We find the defendant guilty," the

---

44. Driver, *Liberating Rites*, 93.

accused was presumed innocent; now the person is a criminal, a convict who will soon be sentenced by the judge. Before the officiant says, "I now pronounce you wed as spouses for life," the two people are single individuals; afterwards, they are a married couple with legally binding responsibilities to and for one another. Before the minister says, "This is my Body, broken for you," the loaf on the table is ordinary bread; afterwards, it is the Body of Christ.

While not all performance is performative in this sense, all performances make something happen. When the mechanic fixes a flat tire, the car can be driven. When an acrobat walks on a thin wire high overhead, people gasp. When a parent hides behind a pillow and then reappears, the baby giggles. Performances may have many purposes: some deceive, some heal, some disclose, some delight. Some might do all of these, and more. So, when singers, actors, musicians, and preachers say that what they do in worship is not performance, they are not rejecting the notion of making something happen. They are asserting that performance has a quality of falseness or inauthenticity that is not appropriate for those who are leading or participating in Christian worship. They seem to equate performing with showing off, with doing something for other people to observe or admire, with acting religious rather than being authentically faithful.

For instance, the authors of *The Work of the People,* a handbook for churches seeking to revitalize their worship practices, write, "Worship is not entertainment, nor is it 'performed' by clergy or professional musicians for the people's benefit."[45] As if in response to the implicit critique, Jana Childers and Clayton Schmit write:

> The very word performance in relation to worship and preaching tends to make some people shiver with anxiety. The word (and the art) is, nonetheless, essential to preaching and other dimensions of worship leadership. . . . Performance does not have to mean "mere performance," or playacting. It is critical to the execution of things, in the way that a surgeon performs life and death medical procedures.[46]

Of course, those who lead worship should not be showing off or doing things for the sake of being watched or admired. But that kind of performing is just as problematic in the theater or the concert hall as it is in church. As Lisa Cole Smith put it:

45. Gilbert et al., *Work of the People,* 10.
46. Childers and Schmit, *Performance in Preaching,* 14.

The last thing that a performer wants to be doing is performing. You want it to be authentic and embodied and true. There is this flip side: in the performance world, or even the entertainment world, the goal is always to be as true as possible. Comedy is only funny if it is coming from a real place.[47]

As noted earlier, "true" in this sense does not necessarily mean "factual" but rather telling people something true about themselves as human beings.

Like performance, acting is another word with ambiguous meaning. To act, in its simplest sense, is to do something, to take action. On the other hand, to act can also mean to portray someone different than oneself, or to pretend to feel differently than one actually does. To act religious, in ordinary speech, means to be a religious hypocrite, one who publicly speaks and acts as though believing in the power of the Risen Christ, for example, while privately rejecting such belief or behaving in unscrupulous, self-serving ways that are inconsistent with that faith. To act religious is to suggest a virtue that does not, in fact, exist.

On the other hand, some performances are meant to delight us with their verisimilitude rather than to deceive. In her book *Acting Religious*, actor, teacher, and theologian Victoria Rue uses this common understanding to underscore a way of thinking about acting and faith:

> "Acting religious" seems to point to artificiality—superficial piety—actions without meaning. With the title of this book my intention is to evoke the image of artificiality in order to ask, what is religious experience? How does intentional action intensify bodily experience? "Acting religious" also seems to suggest that acting is deceiving, lying. Not so. Acting is about entering into another's experience with your own experience and realizing something new from the combustion that occurs.[48]

Rue reflects on the paradox that actors are entirely present to themselves while simultaneously inhabited by the energy and psyche of their characters. She says that this meeting can be so intimate and seamless that it becomes a mystical joining. In recounting the process by which Anna Deavere Smith prepares for the multiple roles that she plays in her solo performances, Rue writes:

47. Smith, interview, 2015.
48. Rue, *Acting Religious*, 8.

Her method is interviewing another with a tape recorder, observing keenly the whole person as she does so (gestures, speech rhythms including ahh's and uh's), transcribing and editing the interview, and memorizing the interview and the physicality of the person.

Rehearsal, practicing over and over, returning to the recorded interview continually, like a touchstone, is Smith's process. What results is Smith's embodied interpretation of another that is also a keen, intuitive observation of that person's core. This mystical joining of self and other is both the challenge and the reward. From this basic process, through the juxtaposition of characters, she tells the multi-voiced, multilayered stories of America.[49]

When Smith finally takes the stage, she is neither exactly herself nor exactly any one of the people she portrays. She is not deceiving anyone, since it is clear that it is the actor, Anna Deavere Smith, who is on stage and who people have paid good money to see. Nor is she telling a made-up story since her words and actions are taken from interviews with real people. Rather, she invites the audience to enter an as-if space, where they simultaneously know that they are witnessing a performance yet feel as if they are in the authentic presence of someone who is not really there. She embodies the "other" in such a way that the audience experiences at one and the same time both the person that she is portraying and the actor who has almost entirely disappeared into her role. That sense of "as if," the "almost," is a critical part of the appreciation of the actor's skill. On leaving the theater, people speak admiringly about a good performance.

The kind of performing that Rue describes, whether in a church or a theater, is not showing off, but rather making something happen. What that "something" is or whether it happens at all depends on the interaction of the performer, the venue, and the willingness of those present to enter into the as-if world.

Clowning Around

In the nineteen-sixties and seventies, there was an exuberant rush to experiment with various forms of worship. Organs and hymns were replaced by guitars and folk songs, banners and other kinds of artwork were brought into previously austere worship spaces, and vestments were made of kente

49. Rue, *Acting Religious*, 102.

cloth or decorated with rainbows to make them appealing to a new generation. In one experiment, dubbed "clown ministry," ministers and other worship leaders donned brightly colored wigs, red noses, and giant shoes, transforming themselves into characters with names like Bubbles, Cheap Grace, or Coppa Plea. While many people find the whole notion of clowns in worship distasteful and disrespectful, for others this kind of creativity and playfulness helps to enliven the worshiping experience and even give it new meaning.

Theologian Katherine Harmon points up this tension, writing of a clown ministry run by the Sisters of Mount St. Benedict, in Erie, Pennsylvania, in the 1980s. Harmon notes that their costumes allowed them to break down barriers that traditional nuns' habits might create and spread the Gospel with a touch of humor:

> Before we judge . . . it is important to note that these same religious sisters from Mount St. Benedict, through the 1970s, had been intensely involved (as so many religious sisters had) with protests for peace and justice: anti-war efforts abroad and civil rights organization at home. For sisters whose lives were so consumed with opposing violence and injustice, the joyful, gentle humor of clown ministry provided balance in their vocation.[50]

Clown ministries like that created by the sisters from Mount St. Benedict continue in many places today, bringing humor and healing to children in oncology wards, elders in nursing homes, and anyone else who needs a smile or maybe a miracle. An essay by Dean Cotton, the clown ministry director of the World Clown Association, explains that clown ministry is not just clowning around:

> Ministry can come in many forms and ministry means different things to each person. I believe that ministry clowning is more than using the art of clowning to deliver a religious message. We minister to people when we meet needs. The need for laughter is universal, but especially to "the least of these," those our busy society has set to the side. So when you clown around in a nursing home, children's home, hospital, disaster zone, homeless shelter, or places like these, you are ministering to their need for smiles and laughter.
>
> Several years ago I was clowning around with the sing along choir for a large group of seniors at a nursing/rehabilitation facility near my home. After we had completed the group time I was asked

50. Harmon, "Legitimate Liturgical Function."

by the staff if DeanO [Cotton's clown persona] had time to visit some residents that were not able to attend the sing along. I visited several people in their rooms, twisted balloon flowers and visited for several minutes. One of the staff was ushering me from room to room. In the last room we visited there was an elderly lady in bed staring out the window. As I twisted a smiley face flower balloon for her, she began to talk to the colorful clown. The staff person suddenly became very excited and exclaimed "I can't believe it! I must get her daughter" (who was in the hall) and she rushed out of the door. The daughter entered and was equally excited. I was not sure what was happening or did happen, but I completed our few minutes together and made my exit. In the hall they explained to me that this lady had not talked to anyone for several weeks. To them it was almost a miracle. But to me it was only a little surprising. It is the ability of a clown to help someone forget the trials and troubles of life, even if for a short time.[51]

There is, of course, a difference between clowns doing ministry in places where people are hurting, and clowns showing up in church to lead worship. Just as the Beyoncé Mass or the light show at the Montreal cathedral drew many disapproving comments, the prospect of clowns in church often raises the scorn of those who expect worship to be decorous and visibly pious. While the clown ministry movement is much smaller than it was in the 1980s, a quick search on the internet suggests that it is still popular in some places, with many scripts available for clowns to use in church services, especially at the children's time and communion. Clowns today continue to appear in worship, to be greeted with both consternation and delight.

A Personal Story

While clowns have recently been receiving some bad press, I have a soft spot for them in worship. One of the most moving eucharistic experiences that I can remember took place in 1990. I was new in town and had only been attending the church in question for a few weeks. Indeed, although I had had a conversion experience about a year earlier and thought of myself as a Christian, I had not yet been baptized. Respecting what I knew about Christian traditions, I refrained from receiving the elements when, as in

51. Cotton, "Don't Neglect Sharing Our Gifts."

many Protestant churches, they celebrated communion on the first Sunday of each month.

Long before the Emerging Church movement, this small, nonde-nominational congregation was highly invested in creative worship and shared leadership. In the long, narrow worship space, chairs were normally arranged in a semicircle facing the cross, altar, and lectern which were grouped in the center along one of the long walls. However, when the appropriate Sunday in Lent came around to celebrate the Lord's Supper, the entire worship space had been rearranged, the lights were dimmed, and all the chairs faced one end of the room, which was curtained off with dark gauze. The altar was behind the curtain, and the lectern had been removed altogether.

At the door, two people dressed as ragged clowns wordlessly handed masks to each person as they entered. Another person, also dressed in artful rags and exaggerated makeup, led the congregation solemnly through the prayers and hymns of the accustomed order of worship. Then we were invited into an extended silence. After several minutes, a procession of clowns elaborately carried in the bread and wine, taking them behind the semitransparent curtain to place them on the altar, and wordlessly prayed the eucharistic prayer. When the bread had been blessed and broken, the clown ushers took people's hands, and led them behind the curtain to receive the elements. As each person emerged on the other side, they no longer wore a mask—instead, they wore a shining star, pasted onto their cheek or forehead. I don't remember what happened after that, because I was weeping. What I knew in that moment was that I needed to be baptized by Easter so that I, too, could receive communion with the rest of the congregation.

This story is offered neither to condemn nor condone clowns at communion or any other worship practice that seems to cross the line from worship to entertainment. Rather, it is an example of how what seems at first glance to be a sharp, bright line can easily blur into a confusing landscape where the boundaries are never quite clear. The following chapter continues to explore this complex terrain with the guidance of actors, preachers, liturgists, and musicians who spend their personal and professional lives in the borderland of worship, entertainment, and the arts.

six

Soli Deo Gloria

Let spectacles, therefore, and plays that are full of vulgar language and of abundant gossip, be forbidden. For what base action is it that is not exhibited in the theatres? And what shameless saying is it that is not brought forward by the buffoons? And those who enjoy the evil that is in them stamp the clear images of it at home. And, on the other hand, those that are proof against these things, and unimpressible, will never cause to stumble in regard to luxurious pleasures.[1]

THE NOTION THAT THERE is something sinful about entertainment has a long history in Christian thought. Some of the earliest writings of the church condemn spectacles and plays as not simply vulgar, but actually evil. Similarly, despite positive mentions in the Hebrew scripture of Miriam dancing in celebration of the Israelites' newfound freedom and David dancing before the Ark of the Covenant, dance has often been seen as an instrument of the devil, enticing people into a dangerous sensuousness. Even music has sometimes been viewed with suspicion, as may be seen in Augustine's famous lament that it is a grievous sin to find the singing itself more moving than the truth of the words. As Lisa Cole Smith puts it,

> I believe the arts were intended as a means to help us address religious questions, our religious act of living. But unfortunately

1. Clement of Alexandria, *Instructor*, III:11.

135

there is a lot of baggage and, in some cases, for legitimate reasons. Performers have been associated with prostitution and with living a very unholy kind of life. And that impression gets carried into the church.[2]

This ongoing fear about the seductive power of the arts, especially those that require the presence of the human body, is the demon that haunts all discussions of performance in the church. When entertainment is demonized as the source of evil in society, then anything that looks like entertainment is banished from congregational worship if not from the everyday lives of Christians. Nevertheless, the church has always relied on the same skills and techniques that make entertainment so compelling in order to enliven worship. This chapter returns to the borderland to listen to the inhabitants talk about some of the ways that entertainment is cast as a tempting demon, and how the same skills and techniques that are at the heart of entertainment can also be used for the glory of God.

Lisa Cole Smith: Is It Worship or a Performance?

Lisa Cole Smith is an actor, director, pastor, and creative entrepreneur in the Washington, DC, area. She received her BFA in drama from Carnegie Mellon University in Pittsburgh and worked as a professional actor for many years before attending seminary and seeking a way to merge her calling as an artist and a person of faith. After receiving her MTS degree from the John Leland Center for Theological Studies in 2006, she founded an experimental church focused on art and artists called Convergence: A Creative Community of Faith.

Smith highlights the difficulty in making hard-and-fast distinctions about worship and entertainment. At her somewhat unconventional church, she reaches out to those who need a church home that will nurture them as artists. When asked what she thought makes the difference between worship and entertainment, she replied:

> I think part of where it gets complex is even in the definition of what worship is. If we are defining worship as a particular time where we do particular things, then that is one thing. If worship is a state of being in relation to God no matter where I am or what I am doing, then it is something else. In my experience, a play, either performing or viewing, could be an act of worship, just

2. Smith, interview, 2015.

as a conversation might be an act of worship. It depends on the approach.[3]

She describes an Advent service at her church in which a group of musicians called the 7 Sopranos performed with virtually no formal prayer or explicit order of worship:

> I think for me, personally, the lines are very, very thin. I think it does have a lot to do with intent. They would do the same thing somewhere else at a different time and that is a concert. When we bring them into a church, during a time we designate as worship, we call it a worship service. So, what is the difference? I think it is about the naming of this time as set apart and sacred, and explicitly saying we are engaging in worship together. At our church, we talk about training for "whole-life worship": our whole, everyday existence can be—and ultimately, we would want it to be—acts or experiences of worship.[4]

Smith says that there is something special about gathering as a community and choosing to engage in a specific act of worship together, while noting that her community interprets what a worship service is very broadly. She defines worship not as specific actions, but as an intention to be aware of the presence of God:

> I think when the elements chosen are intended to help people turn towards God, and the hearts and minds of those involved are turned towards God together, then we are engaged in worship.[5]

Smith acknowledges that there are certain pieces of music that may be inappropriate or even completely opposed to a worshipful experience. Nevertheless, she insists that secular music that addresses the human condition can have an important role in connecting people with the divine. Even when the musicians come from other religious traditions, for Smith it is the intention of the gathering that matters. When people enter a place of worship and know that worship is the reason for being there, then it *is* worship, even if what happens might look like something else.

Reflecting on her own experience as a person of faith in the theater world, Smith remembers that early in her career, she felt her performance was about herself, what she was doing, how she looked, and how she came

3. Smith, interview, 2015.

4. Smith, interview, 2015.

5. Smith, interview, 2015.

across as an actor. Later, as she began to pray for the Holy Spirit to use the experience in some way, acting itself became for her a form of worship:

> There was a difference in the way I approached it and the way that I saw my role. And, I think, honestly, it made me a better actor. I think it got me closer to what it really means to be an actor. It was immaturity on my part to make it about me. Because acting is about embodiment. I learned to pray to be open and prepared to embody the character and become a vessel for whatever God would do through me. I recognized that regardless of what happened on stage, something else often happened in the space between the stage and the audience. Sometimes a performance that I did not think went very well would be incredibly meaningful to someone else. And there would be performances when I felt, Oh I did such a good job, I nailed it! And it didn't really do anything for anybody else.[6]

Smith came to understand that to be a performer is to become a vessel for the divine to pour through, giving something to other people through her performance. She now believes that actors, musicians, and other performers are designed to be that kind of vessel, and that worship in her church can allow them the space to do what God intends them to do.

When asked what part of her acting self she brings to her preaching, she says:

> There is the training in how to speak; to be loud enough and to be visible, that kind of thing. But I think my training also has given me a meaningful approach to reading Scripture in a way that is really trying to bring it to life, giving each word the space and the fullness that it needs. I think I am able to do that because I approach it the way I approach a script. There is something in here that is meaty and interesting and needs to be given life and color, so I use my voice and pauses and inflections in order to give that space. I think that is probably also true in the way that I speak, in allowing the personal-ness and the passion of it to come out. I'm sure the fact that I'm trained as an actor makes me more comfortable in front of a group of people. But then it gets back to the conversation about authenticity verses inauthenticity. I'm not getting up there and acting, but like I said before, I wouldn't get up on stage and "act" either. I think my acting training helps me to be

---

6. Smith, interview, 2015.

more authentic, gives me more of a desire to convey trueness, and allow parts of my inner-vulnerable self to show through.[7]

Smith notes that some people assume that because she is an actor, she must be good at being false and manipulative. On the contrary, she insists, manipulating a group to do something or to experience something particular is not the intent of either actor or pastor. Although preachers actually do want a certain response to their sermons, choosing words and images and pacing carefully in order to get it, that is not manipulation in the nefarious, backhanded sense of the word. Smith tells the following story as an explanation:

> I went to a college where drama students and computer programming students were in close proximity to one another on campus. Some male programmer friends once told me they were wary of girls in the drama department because "how would you ever know whether or not she was lying?" That surprised and insulted me for a number of reasons. Equating acting with lying, to me, didn't make sense. Lying is about masking self and trying to deceive, whereas acting is about laying oneself bare and trying to reveal truth. It seems to me that loaded ideas about performing don't have anything to do with the art form itself but are confused with questions about the character of the individuals doing the performing. That, I think, is what needs to get separated when you have this conversation about performance or entertainment verses worship.[8]

Smith questions the premise that entertainment is less valuable than performances that are called by the loftier title of art. For her, even entertainment can be a conduit to help people fulfill a need to laugh, to escape, to experience something they had not experienced before in a way that is nonthreatening. For her, both entertainment and art are powerful, meaningful experiences that are given to us by God and that can be done in a worshipful manner.

Ken Fong: Narrative Preaching

Ken Fong is well-known in the Asian American Christian community as a courageous pastor, teacher, thinker, and a leading progressive voice

7. Smith, interview, 2015.
8. Smith, interview, 2015.

among American Baptists and other evangelicals. Fong recently retired after twenty-one years as the senior pastor of Evergreen Baptist Church of Los Angeles (now in Rosemead, California), a large pan-Asian, multi-ethnic congregation. He now serves as affiliate associate professor of Asian American church studies at Fuller Theological Seminary. A proponent of narrative preaching, Fong tells his students,

> It's a sin to be boring. I say, God is not boring, the Gospel is not boring, so if people think God or the Gospel is boring, that is on you.[9]

Fong's own preaching style is casual, confident, and engaging. Walking around the congregation with a wireless mic, he tells stories out of his own life, connecting personal insights and observations about contemporary society with the larger biblical imperatives to love God and neighbor, to seek justice and do kindness, and to follow Jesus as lord and savior.

Fong also hosts a weekly podcast that explores the cultural, artistic, historical, and spiritual aspects of the Asian-American community, cultivating relationships with many members of the entertainment industry. Recently he was invited to participate at a first-timers session at a local comedy festival. When invited to reflect on the difference between preaching and stand-up comedy, he related his conversation with the organizer:

> It is one thing for people to think you have a sense of humor. It is another thing for people to expect you to be funny the entire five minutes. I said [to the organizer], "But try this: for thirty minutes, they are also supposed to hear from God." I said, "That's more pressure, not just to make people laugh, but somehow through this earthen vessel they're going to hear from God."[10]

Describing his own preaching, Fong says that he uses observational humor to get people laughing and disarm them so that they are set up for something more serious and meaningful:

> I use humor a lot, in a way that is more like Seinfeld. It is more observational humor. Do you ever think about "this," right? And I get people laughing to disarm them and then it sets them up for something more serious and meaningful.[11]

9. Fong, interview, 2015.
10. Fong, interview, 2015.
11. Fong, interview, 2015.

After his stand-up debut, Fong asked his wife what she thought. He relates that after praising his effort, she cautioned,

> "I want you to know two things: number one, you have an opportunity that most of those comics don't have on a weekly basis, of standing in front of an audience of people who are willing to listen. You have been able to work on this for a long time. They would kill to have the opportunities that you have." But, she said, "more importantly, when I've heard you use humor in your sermons, it still has a meaningful point. And tonight, that wasn't required of you and so I felt something was missing."[12]

As Fong discovered, there is a difference between a preacher and a stand-up comic. It is not that a preacher cannot and should not be entertaining, but rather that there is more to preaching than simple entertainment. As he insists to his students, preachers should never be boring. However, he cautions, entertaining the congregation must never become more important than helping them understand what it means to live as a member of the Body of Christ.

Heather Murray Elkins: Preaching as a Performing Art

Heather Murray Elkins is professor of worship, preaching, and the arts at the Theological School of Drew University in Madison, New Jersey, and an ordained elder in the West Virginia Annual Conference of the United Methodist Church. Her courses include sacramental preaching, worship, narrative theology, ritual, and Appalachian studies. Her Youtube series, *Holy Stuff of Life*, is based on storytelling, object relations and the Christian year.

The tensions and similarities between preaching and performance are also important to Elkins as she works with seminarians. To illuminate her understanding of the relationship between worship and entertainment, Elkins described an assignment for a course called "Preaching and the Performing Arts" in which students struggled with definitions of preaching, proclamation, and performance. When I asked about it, she said:

> "Preaching and the Performing Arts" grew out of an earlier course on ministry and imagination. What we discovered moving into the course was that what seminary students needed the most to

12. Fong, interview, 2015.

work on was their bodies. It was as if they had so disciplined themselves that all of it was from the neck up. We needed scholars of the body. We were able to bring in people who were body-articulate and could train people to even identify themselves as body.[13]

Elkins notes that an important question at the beginning was how to teach people to fail so they would learn from that failing, from doing something that they were not already good at. To address that question, the class was offered only as pass/fail, and the way to fail was not to be fully emotionally and intellectually present. Elkins also reasoned that students will take any class with the word "preaching" in it, because they feel somehow that is what the church really needs them to do.

As the new course developed, Elkins invited a Drew graduate who was also a dancer with an international reputation to team-teach with her. On the first day of class, they asked students to write a response to the question "preaching is performance—true, false? Do you have trouble with these two words together?" Elkins notes that for some students,

> performance was a negative word. "I want to preach, so it is not a performance." Other students were liturgical dancers, so they had problems with the word preaching. "Well, I dance but I don't preach." They had problems from another perspective, "My dance is dance." I could move them to the idea that it was proclamation. That was middle ground. But the idea that it was in fact a form of preaching, that took more time. . . . We start with recognizing the difficulty of fitting those two words together and the fact that performance is almost always used as the word to damn a sermon. "He was just performing, she was just acting." It was inauthentic, contrived, manipulative, all those words. We wrote those words out. Then, when they were reading their responses, that is what the board fills up with. You look at this, you can even take a picture if you want, and at the end of the course we'll look at it again.[14]

Students in the class were required to do both a sermon and a performance. Elkins relates one student's very dramatic sermon:

> They were all assigned to either preach or perform out of Jeremiah, two passages, the potter's house and the smashing of the [clay jar]. There was one student who preached the entire sermon while walking around, holding this jar. Of course, at the end, as

13. Elkins, interview, 2017.
14. Elkins, interview, 2017.

she is getting angrier and angrier in her proclamation, denuncia-
tion—they are not listening, they are not listening—she smashes
it in the chapel.[15]

When it came time for the other students to evaluate what had occurred, it was clear that they were troubled. Elkins relates their horrified
responses to a sermon that ended with such a strong sense of judgment,
noting, "It was as if they could have handled it better in a performance
because it was 'only' a performance. But that it was a sermon!"[16]

This strong reaction indicates that for Elkins' students, at least, there
is an expectation that a sermon must end on a note of hope, whereas a
performance can end in destruction. Although it is clear that the students
were profoundly moved, and perhaps even convicted, by the unexpected
smashing of the clay vessel at the end of the sermon, it is also clear that they
thought that some kind of line had been crossed between preaching and
performance.

Thomas G. Long: From Spectacle to Authenticity

Thomas G. Long is Bandy Professor Emeritus of Preaching and Director
of the Early Career Pastoral Leadership Program at Emory University's
Candler School of Theology. He is an ordained minister in the Presbyterian
Church (USA), served as the senior homiletics editor of *The New Interpreter's Bible*, and is associate editor of *Journal for Preachers* and editor-at-large
for *The Christian Century*.

Long is widely acknowledged as an important voice in the world of
homiletics. When asked about current concerns about worship becoming
too much like entertainment, he reminded me that there were similar concerns in the fourth century. As he tells the story,

> Augustine was a dazzlingly attractive orator, and people jammed
> into the church in Hippo to hear him. In one of his sermons he
> says, "I want to speak to the pagans for a moment. I know why you
> are here. You are here for spectacle. Well, we have one. It is called
> Eucharist." And then he teaches about the drama of the Eucharist
> itself. I think there is a dramatic production quality to good wor-
> ship. We are in a Christian tragicomedy that we act out every week,
> acting authentically, recognizing that these make-believe roles are

15. Elkins, interview, 2017.
16. Elkins, interview, 2017.

also our real lives, our real roles as well, but we are imaginatively dress-rehearsing who we will be at the Great Feast.[17]

Coming back to the current situation, he refers to philosopher Martha Nussbaum's comparison between Greek drama and Broadway theater:

> She says that in Broadway theater we sit in a darkened auditorium and watch actors and actresses on an illuminated stage doing the latest play. In Greek drama, the stage is in the middle of the village in broad daylight. The village gathers around and everybody has a part. At some point you get up out of your seat and you get on stage and speak your lines. It is a play that has been done many times before because it is the central values of the culture. In that sense, Christian worship is more like Greek drama than it is like Broadway theater. A rock concert or pure entertainment venue is probably more like Broadway theater.[18]

While Long concedes that audiences do get involved in Broadway plays, rock concerts, and performances of Shakespeare, the difference is that in worship everyone has a role in the drama that is being played out:

> In worship you are not simply watching and being involved as an observer, with whatever degree of emotional connection. You are actually in the play. That doesn't mean you are necessarily the preacher or the presider at the table or the band or the choir.[19]

Preachers do have a special role in worship. Long teaches his students not to be afraid of the word performance. He compares the experience of giving the same sermon three times in a row on a Sunday morning to that of an actor in a play in a long run. Just as the actor is not surprised by anything in the script by the six hundredth performance, preachers are not always breathtakingly caught up in their own words. Nevertheless, Long says,

> you can perform that for a congregation. You are playing the role of a proclaimer of the Gospel and your emotional state comes and goes in regard to that. But you do so as an act of faith and will. You are loyal to that role even when your emotions don't always trail along. Now if you never had any emotional involvement, there would be something wrong. But when I preach at eight o'clock and

17. Long, interview, 2015.
18. Long, interview, 2015.
19. Long, interview, 2015.

tell a story in a sermon, I have a different feeling about that story than when I tell it at eleven for the third time to a new congregation. I have to draw deep on a reservoir to put energy into that retelling, so that at eleven o'clock it is as much of a gift as it was at eight o'clock.[20]

For Long, this kind of performance is no different from that of a conductor of a symphony orchestra whose task it is to give the audience the composer's musical ideas, being faithful to the score and to the event of conducting a particular piece of music. Similarly, a preacher's job is to interpret Scripture and preach the Gospel, being faithful to the text and to the event of preaching.

The danger is that, just as going to a rock concert is at least as much being in the presence of the performer as it is about the music itself, sometimes a preacher's persona can become more important than the Word of God, both to the preacher and to the listeners. In the nineteenth century, styles of preaching changed from using grand gestures and big words to a more intimate, conversational tone as people began to distrust the distance between public and private personas. Charles Finney, for example,

began to realize as an evangelist that if he would talk in the pulpit like he talked at home, he suddenly had a congregation galvanized. And instead of a big gesture, he perfected the little gesture. Fred Craddock did the same thing in the 1970s and '80s. Instead of the big voice, it is the little voice. Instead of the grandiloquent sermon, the homespun story, the yarn-oriented sermon. And suddenly, Finney introduced into homiletical vocabulary the words "authenticity" and "sincerity." People would say, I don't believe a word he says, but he's so sincere! And it is powerful.[21]

Over time, other preachers began to imitate Finney's sincere style, not noticing the irony of imitation sincerity. Indeed, a sincere style can be used to mask poor theology and or to manipulate listeners. While today it is often assumed that authenticity in the pulpit has always been important, it came as a welcome surprise to listeners who were more used to the practiced rhetorical flourishes that Augustine defended in the fourth century.

20. Long, interview, 2015.
21. Long, interview, 2015.

Heather Josselyn-Cranson: Full, Conscious, Active Participation

Heather Josselyn-Cranson holds the Sister Margaret William McCarthy Endowed Chair in Music at Regis College, a Catholic university in greater Boston. Josselyn-Cranson teaches in the fields of music and religion, including classes on the New Testament, spiritual autobiographies, music and health, and ethnomusicology. She also directs the Regis Chamber Singers and the Regis Glee Singers. Her scholarship focuses on the intersection of music and worship, both in modern-day Emerging Church contexts as well as in the medieval monastic context of the Order of Sempringham.

As a musician and liturgical scholar, Josselyn-Cranson thinks a great deal about the role of music in congregational life. When asked about the difference between worship and entertainment, she said that her first thought was that entertainment is passive and worship needs to be full, conscious, active participation. On later consideration, however, she realized that although our cultural assumption is that entertainment is largely passive, activities as diverse and as fully engaging as roller-coasters, travel, and dancing are generally classed as entertainment.

As a way to approach the question from a different direction, Josselyn-Cranson mentions the frequently heard concern about getting young people to engage in worship rather than goofing off or checking out. At the invitation of one of her students, she visited a church that was holding an evening event for middle and high school students. The event started with dinner, followed by a worship service that began with music videos being projected, not only on the screen, but all around the room. The videos were relatively contemporary in style, with lyrics that were Christian-appropriate and age-appropriate. However, Josselyn-Cranson reports, the videos were very atmospheric and style-conscious, even featuring some provocative clothing. As the lighting changed, a smoke machine started to send smoke billowing out from the stage area into the audience. Noting that "stage" and "audience" are appropriate terms for that particular architectural space, Josselyn-Cranson relates that someone whom she assumed was the youth program director came out to talk with the young people:

> He says, "We're really glad you are here. We want you just as you are. If you've never been to this before, that is OK. We don't want you to change yourselves. Don't change anything. Stay just as you are. We want you to be comfortable." The students are hearing the sounds, they are watching the videos, they are being told to be

comfortable, and then the band starts playing. "Stand up, come on, sing out! Let's hear it! Get involved!" It struck me that these young people were just being given two contradictory messages. Number one, don't change, be absolutely comfortable, relax; number two, give one hundred percent of who you are to Jesus in this very moment.[22]

As Josselyn-Cranson reflected on these contradictory messages, it seemed to her that the leaders saw being relaxed and entertained as somehow problematic at the same time as the setting encouraged exactly that:

> Most people watch music videos for entertainment. The smoke machine is so often used with shows that we tend to watch more passively. We tend to watch or listen to, rather than participate or sing or perform in or with them. And certainly this space speaks. The band is up higher, at the front; everyone is pointed toward the band; they are lit. The entire congregation is seated in the darkness, not able to see one another, very difficult to hear one another. All of that power differential allows congregation members to sink into a more passive and entertainment posture. [23]

It is not only the rock-concert, music-video style that encourages passivity, however. Many more traditional approaches to worship also allow congregations to simply be present, perhaps allowing the waves of beautiful music to wash over them without any further involvement on their part than if they were at a symphony hall. After all, many people, both those who go to church regularly and those who never attend, will say that they have profound spiritual experiences at concerts where well-trained choirs sing very difficult, very beautiful music.

Josselyn-Cranson argues for a more active kind of participation in church services. Rather than providing entertainment, she believes that the prime function of a church choir is to support the singing of the congregation. Acknowledging that this may not be communicated well to most people, she nevertheless insists that congregational singing is primary and that the choir is there to help guide the congregation through communion responses or sung prayer, or to create a more textured harmony while the congregation's melody rests above it. Choirs may also sing an anthem that is more challenging musically than a congregation can manage, and this is where active listening comes in. For Josselyn-Cranson, when the congregation listens actively,

22. Josselyn-Cranson, interview, 2016.
23. Josselyn-Cranson, interview, 2016.

the choir's performance would not be as much of a show to be appreciated or to entertain the congregation, but would be almost a dialogical event where there is active attention on both sides to singing this music and then to wrestling and grappling with this music, asking "What does it mean for us as the Body of Christ right now?"[24]

Josselyn-Cranson believes that active listening involves paying attention to the meaning of the music, what the sounds themselves convey beyond the words of the text. There may be things that the composer did not intend, things that are very difficult to specify in words, yet are important to acknowledge and wrestle with. Listening in this way can help congregations ask,

> What does this mean for us today? What does this mean for us in the context of Epiphany, or Holy Week, or the loss of our ninety-two-year-old beloved matriarch in the congregation, or whatever the church is going through? I think in the context of the Body of Christ, in the context of the congregation, the meaning has to be understood as related to the scriptures, the prayers, the sacraments being celebrated, such that somehow that piece of music is part of the liturgy. There is a lot of synthesizing to be done.[25]

Of course, most congregations are not educated to listen in this way. For active listening to occur, congregations need to know that the choir director didn't choose this anthem just because he or she likes it, but because it reflects upon something else in the service. Josselyn-Cranson believes that leaders can help congregations do far more in assuming their active role in bringing together the various parts of worship, which might help them take one step away from treating worship as entertainment.

Geoffrey C. Moore: Liturgy as a Narrative Form

Geoffrey C. Moore is a PhD candidate at Southern Methodist University's Dedman College of Humanities and Science, where his work has focused on sacramental theology and on examining the intersection of music and theology. Moore serves as the president of the Hymn Society in the United States and Canada and is a commissioned elder in the North Texas Conference of the United Methodist Church.

24. Josselyn-Cranson, interview, 2016.
25. Josselyn-Cranson, interview, 2016.

When asked to articulate his understanding of the relationship between good worship and good entertainment, Moore notes that there is a great deal of similarity, particularly in the sense that both have as their goal the exploration and adoration of beauty. The difference is that in worship, there is the additional meaning of beauty as an attribute of God. Still, as for Gordon Lathrop, the primary difference that Moore sees between worship and entertainment is in the audience:

> The audience for entertainment is generally anthropocentric. That is, we are the audience for entertainment. It is a human-to-human endeavor, whereas liturgy is theocentric. In some sense the audience is God, and this is a God-human endeavor. All of those roles around who is acting, who is the audience, who is on stage—all of them shift around. I think of entertainment as falling more into the category of the Baroque category of divertissement, which delights in the sense of diverting attention away from other mundane things. Entertainment does not necessarily reflect attention in a theocentric way, whereas liturgy delights in a way that intends to edify and divert attention towards God.[26]

Moore has directed community chorales as well as church choirs for many years. He critiques the typical format of a choral concert as inhuman because even those which are organized around a theme tend to have a static, nonnarrative quality. Arguing that narrative is basic to human communication, memory, and relationship, he says that audience members have to work too hard to understand and relate to one standalone piece after another. On the other hand, art forms such as opera, theater, or even ballet are generally grounded in continuous narrative, as is much of what is usually thought of as entertainment.

Most Protestant worship services, Moore says, are more like choral concerts, in which it is difficult to discern any story line. He likens such services to paint-by-numbers, in which

> we do a hymn and then we do a creed and then we do a Scripture reading and then we do another hymn and then we do a closing hymn and then we do a benediction. What would any of those things have to do with each other, except that maybe today the theme is love? Or today the theme is forgiveness, and all of these things have to do with forgiveness. But if the pattern is based on the Mass and the Mass is a dramatic structure, then the pattern must also tell a story from entering into God's presence to experiencing

26. Moore, interview, 2016.

God's grace again to being called to repentance, or whatever that story is in any particular tradition. And I think that we can use the arts and entertainment to help us think more deeply into what liturgical structure is going on and make that more humane and less like a choral concert.[27]

For Moore, both good entertainment and good worship are grounded in narrative. When both are done well, it is possible to say that good liturgy is good theater and good theater is good liturgy. The liturgy leads the congregation through a narrative story of salvation, redemption, and reconciliation; good theater leads into a deeper sense of awe, of the other, and of beauty. Similarly,

the arts tend to not let symbols or visual images be static or haphazard or inadvertent. In well-crafted entertainment, whether that is an opera or a play or a ballet or a musical piece or a film, all of the imagery—the color palette of the costumes or of a scene—will be carefully controlled and intentional.[28]

In liturgy, however, there is little intentionality about the imagery, allowing it to become stale or even extraneous and haphazard. The cross is present, or water, or bread, or wine, but they are not intentionally drawn into the narrative:

We go to great, elaborate work to decorate the altar for Epiphany or World Communion Sunday or whatever, but then that image is just left there. That strong visual is just left for everyone to figure out. Nothing is ever said about the particular images or colors. The symbology that we have put into it is not woven into the rest of the liturgy. It just sits there. That would never happen in any good cinematography.[29]

Like Mark Miller, Moore would like the church to learn more about intentionality from the arts and entertainment world. Rather than simply putting a pretty background behind song lyrics or a sermon, worship should be more like good entertainment, using the arts to strengthen its narrative quality.

---

27. Moore, interview, 2016.
28. Moore, interview, 2016.
29. Moore, interview, 2016.

Roy Barber: Theater as Worship

Roy Barber is a musician, playwright, and teacher. He works with the Bo-kamoso Youth Center, a nonprofit organization in Winterveldt township in South Africa. Bokamoso helps young people at risk learn to be contributing members of society and finish their schooling. For a number of years, Barber has helped a group of singers, dancers, and actors from Bokamoso come to the US every January to perform a musical based on stories drawn from their own lives and to acquire skills that will help them find meaningful work when they return to their homes.

Barber says that, whether in the theater or in worship, the most important thing is to engage the people, bringing them into what is being created. For instance, it is important to anticipate whether something like a loud guitar or some other sound will alienate the audience or excite them and bring them to a new place:

> If you are going to create a meaningful drama, or a meaningful worship piece, you have to find a way in that engages your listeners. You are going to start with them here and you are going to take them somewhere else. I suppose the major difference would be thematic, where the journey is taking your audience.[30]

While contemporary services may be helpful for some people, Barber says that he wants something different in church than what he can hear on the radio. However, the skills that an artist learns to engage a group of people are the same whether it is in service of a comedy show on television or presenting something in a more sacred context. The difference, for him, is the content and how that may be seen as a sacred expression.

For Barber, performance is a way to help people reimagine what the world is or can be. When the young people from Bokamoso perform in the US, it is often, but not always, in the context of Christian worship. When Barber was asked about how those performances differed, he replied:

> We rehearse a lot so that the quality can be as high as possible, but they are different venues. It depends on the space, actually. If you have a proscenium stage and the audience is far away from you, that is a different experience than if you are in a church and people are much closer to you. How you address the congregation, the audience, depends on what space you have and how it fits into the service or the performance. Some of our performance venues

30. Barber, interview, 2015.

when the South African youth are here are clearly more like a theater, so you have the opportunity to use lighting and other special effects that you might not have in a worship service.[31]

Recalling the worship experiences of his own youth, Barber notes that everything had a rhetorical purpose. Whether it was the sermon, the familiar hymns, or anything else,

> all of it was leading to a catharsis where the person in the congregation would be urged to be reborn, which was a very big, life-changing event. Every week the question was, how are we going to change the lives of these people? Will we reach them in a way that they feel guilty, or they feel whatever it is that they need to, to want to change, to make a new decision about what their lives are? I guess there was a very theatrical propaganda tone to the whole service. You walk in and everything contributes to this. There is an in-group of people who know the songs, and if you participate and learn the songs and listen to the minister and understand that you've sinned, and you need to be born again, it will work. It is all going toward this effect.[32]

Barber attends a very different kind of church now and has spent many years teaching musical theater to high school students as well as developing his own projects. Today he is less interested in pure entertainment than he is in worship of a different kind, where the line often blurs between the two. His latest play explores relationships between aging parents and adult children, attempting to reach into deep places in himself and in the audience so their world can be changed or seen differently. In some ways, this is not different from the intentions of the churches in which he grew up, although with a different theology and a different style. Reflecting his understanding that theater is one of the oldest forms of church, he feels it important to bring his own gifts as a performer and director into the service of Christian worship. Similarly, when he produces one of his own plays, he hopes that people will be moved and have a spiritual experience.

Ruth Duck: Love, Care, and Excellence

Ruth Duck recently retired as professor of worship at Garrett-Evangelical Theological Seminary, where she was on the faculty since 1989. She was

31. Barber, interview, 2015.
32. Barber, interview, 2015.

president of the North American Academy of Liturgy, an organization of liturgical scholars, in 2007. She has written many books and articles about Christian worship, as well as numerous hymn texts that are found in the various denominational hymnals. Her 2013 book, *Worship for the Whole People of God: Vital Worship for the 21st Century*, is widely used as a text in courses on worship.

As a hymnwriter and liturgical scholar, Duck has influenced countless pastors and choir directors. Rather than reply directly to a question about worship and entertainment, she recalled a passage from the 1978 statement by the Bishops' Committee on the Liturgy called *Environment and Art in Catholic Worship*, which held up the importance of the "love and care in the making of things." It is not so much the perfection of the artwork that matters in worship, Duck pointed out, but rather giving one's best.

Duck's particular concern is congregational song. While she is unwilling to categorically say that there is no place for praise bands, she does find it problematic when a band is so loud that the congregation cannot find its own voice:

> In that case, entertainment is not enough because it takes the voice and song of the people and makes it belong only to the ensemble. I am not saying there should not be times for people who are well-trained in music—whether classical or contemporary or whatever the style. An anthem sung by a choir, a prelude by the organist, or a bell choir can inspire and uplift the congregation. But the voice of the congregation is most important because we are singing together as well as building a repertoire of songs done together. We learn words and songs that can comfort us when we are troubled, inspire us to love and serve in the week to come, and form a wholesome theology.[33]

This, she points out, is not a new problem. First Church Cambridge was established in 1636, and for the next 150 years or so the only music was psalms and Isaac Watts hymns, sung a cappella. Toward the end of the eighteenth century, First Church got its first organ:

> It was a major event when First Church purchased an organ. Their long-time pastor gave a long, wonderful sermon explaining why they shouldn't just sing a cappella. There was also a big fuss in the church over having a choir, because these Congregational and Puritan Christians feared that the choir would usurp the

---

33. Duck, interview, 2016.

congregation's place. One thing they did to encourage the congregation was to have the choir sit in the back rows so that they would assist the congregation in their singing, but they would not be on show.[34]

Like the early congregations at First Church, Duck believes that the congregation's song should be supported, rather than undermined by organ music that is too loud, as well as music that is not accessible to the congregation. An important role of musicians is to help the congregation learn new songs, as well as coordinating songs with pastors and other worship planners and leaders:

> Once I belonged to a church where the musician was only playing the same two or three songs from the classical repertoire as a prelude every week, without having any relation to the rest of worship. The pastor tried to work with this organist, but he refused to give more love and care for the congregation's worship—however skillful he was at playing this classical music. The pastor eventually had to fire this gifted musician.[35]

As a hymnwriter, it is important to Duck to make the text and tune fit in regular ways, so that the people do not have to sing a different rhythm in every stanza or get confused by technical details that they cannot follow. Church choirs, since they are often made up of members who may not have much musical instruction, can also find some music difficult. For this reason, many churches engage professional section leaders, either all the time or for particular events. Duck remembers that she first encountered this when she was working as a temporary preacher in the Boston area:

> One church had section leaders. It seemed a bit strange to me, because I had never experienced this in the South or Midwest (where I had lived before). At one point, we were singing *Messiah* around Christmas time, and it did not hurt at all to have paid section leaders. One benefit of highly trained musicians is that they are able to give their gifts in in order to bring forth the gifts of the congregation.[36]

There is a spirituality about performance in worship that transcends technical excellence. When the choices become a matter of the preferences

34. Duck, interview, 2016.

35. Duck, interview, 2016.

36. Duck, interview, 2016.

of musicians or their need to show off or to compete with other musicians, it does not contribute to worship. For Ruth Duck, excellence in worship is about the love and care that all the participants put into it. The point is to help the worship experience and the Christian discipleship of the congregation.

Eileen Guenther: Excellent Performance

Eileen Guenther is professor of church music at Wesley Theological Seminary, where she teaches music and worship courses and serves as director of chapel music. A church musician, teacher, scholar, and conductor, she is also three-term president of the American Guild of Organists. Her publications include *Rivals or a Team: Clergy-Musician Relationships in the Twenty-First Century* and *In Their Own Words: Slave Life and the Power of Spirituals*. When asked about the relationship between worship and entertainment, her reply quickly turned to notions of performance. Noting that what used to be a norm in terms of music in worship is no longer possible, she continued,

> I do know for sure that it has to do with the spirit that I, as a performer, bring and the spirit that you, as a worshiper, bring. But it is a two-way street. It is very easy to project motives on someone else. If I say, "Oh, that is a performance," that is an automatic negative because I am assuming that you are there for you rather than either for God or for the greater community. . . . I think anything we do in worship is a performance in the most broad sense of the term. A preacher is performing; a scripture reader is performing. Everyone is bringing their gifts for the greater good. I like to use the word "performance" with a little p, not a big P.[37]

Guenther points out that whether the music comes from a robed choir with a magnificent pipe organ, a contemporary praise band, or a single soloist singing without accompaniment, it is very easy to say that they are doing it to show off their talents or to entertain, with the implication that entertainment is not a good thing. This kind of projection of motives is a perennial problem, as it is impossible to know what is in the performer's heart.

For Guenther, part of the issue is the way that our society, and therefore the church, thinks about and rewards excellence. Too often, people

37. Guenther, interview, 2016.

seem to think that excellent musicians should be performing in a concert hall rather than exercising their gifts in a church setting. On the other hand, a church setting can work against excellence because rehearsal time is limited or other resources are lacking. Nevertheless, excellence in worship is important, Guenther says, because

> excellence allows the Holy Spirit to speak through the music, and something less than excellence can get in the way. This is not saying that you have to have a beautiful voice or a wonderful technique, but rather that, if things don't go well, whatever "well" is in your context—if you are not doing it to the best of your ability and to the best of some kind of an agreed standard, it can get in the way of people being able to appreciate what it is you are bringing.[38]

Guenther is careful to qualify the notion of standards, pointing out that a singer who doesn't necessarily sing on pitch but has the right spirit can be very moving:

> I have plenty of colleagues who would say, "We have an excellent God, and God deserves excellent worship, excellent music," whatever the definition of "excellent" is. But your definition and mine may or may not be the same. And mine may not be the same from one time to another. Whatever the spirit of the service is, I think excellence is contextual.[39]

Nevertheless, while the Holy Spirit can override mistakes, excellence does matter. Guenther is clear that excellence in performance of any kind requires preparation:

> There are a lot of unknowns in performance art. I think that as a solo performer I can corral those unknowns in way that I cannot as a conductor. I can deal with my emotions, with my technical preparation, with getting to know the instrument if it is an organ or a piano, doing my practice and studying the score in a way that prepares me to bring the music to the people.[40]

That preparation differs when she is playing with or conducting a group. In both cases, there is historical and contextual research to be done, as well as examining the music itself in order to make that happen most

38. Guenther, interview, 2016.
39. Guenther, interview, 2016.
40. Guenther, interview, 2016.

beautifully and most faithfully. If the work is in another language, that adds another layer of practice, learning how to pronounce the words accurately:

> The unknowns in a group are vastly multiplied. You have moods and desires and talent and scheduling, all to bring into some kind of cohesion. It takes a lot of sheer luck or genius to choose music that will allow the singers to do their best. Being a steward of people's talent is a prime obligation of someone who does what I do. I want to enable people to do what they can. This may mean the voicing of the piece, the technical difficulty, or the rehearsal time. If I have a lot of rehearsal time, I can choose something a little more challenging. It is my job, as a conductor, to make sure that everyone feels that their contribution is not going to be replaced by a number of other people, that they have something unique to contribute—which in fact they do, because every voice is different and every spirit is different.[41]

Clearly, Guenther believes that it is a director's responsibility to develop the skills of each member of the choir. Planning is an element of this kind of responsibility. While there is a difference between entertainment and a worship service, those who plan a theatrical event have a script or storyboard so that everyone knows what is happening next. Planning how people get from one place to another in the worship space is often ignored until the moment when someone who has been turning pages for the pianist at the far right is expected to read Scripture from the lectern at the far left, and the congregation has nothing to do but watch an awkward walk across the sanctuary. Instead, as in entertainment, all the elements of a worship service need to work together and be thought about in preparation for the event. For instance, Guenther confesses,

> I am really bothered by discontinuity of subject matter. Having a sermon preached on a certain subject and having something diametrically opposed immediately following it musically is fingernails on the blackboard for me. There might be a way to make it work, but what it really screams is, "We didn't ever talk about what we are doing."[42]

Planning, whether it is about the music or about any other element of worship, is what makes excellence possible. The notion of excellence extends to the choices that are made long before the first note of the prelude

---

41. Guenther, interview, 2016.

42. Guenther, interview, 2016.

is played. For Guenther, as for Ruth Duck, excellence has to do with love and care.

Guenther echoes Josselyn-Cranson's concern about the lack of congregational awareness of why one song or another is placed within a service. This is particularly important when the song comes from a different culture than that of the majority of the congregation, lest it become simply a trendy bit of ethno-tourism. If there is something in the bulletin, announcements, or even the sermon that mentions the intention to connect with a certain part of the world or to remember some particular event, then the singing becomes, in Guenther's phrase, "the world's music for the sake of the world." It becomes a moment of prayer with people in a distant land, rather than only for the congregation that is singing.

This is true whether the music is congregational song or a choir anthem. Guenther relies on anthems to do what congregational song cannot. She notes that the standard answer about anthems is that you can worship in a lot of different ways. Music does many things, she says:

> You are not always the person who is going to be doing the performing. Singing on behalf of the congregation is the standard response, and for a very long time, as far back as the time of the Hebrew Scriptures, choirs have been set aside to do special things, to rehearse in a way that the rest of the congregation doesn't have the time, the talent, or the desire to do. It is not something that we just invented. It is something that may feel anachronistic in 2016, but there are congregations that thrive totally on the sung, robed choir experience, and the congregation does not have a lot to do except experience it through what has been prepared on their behalf.[43]

That kind of worship is not for everyone, or perhaps not for every Sunday. While some people might consider a service dominated by the choir more entertainment than worship, Guenther points out that there is a place for all forms of praise. Everyone is called to use their talents for the good of the whole community. To do less than your very best, she says, is not good stewardship.

43. Guenther, interview, 2016.

Cláudio Carvalhaes: At Play in the House of God

Cláudio Carvalhaes is associate professor of worship at Union Theological Seminary in New York, an ordained teaching elder in the Presbyterian Church (U.S.A.), and a much-sought-after speaker, writer, performer, and consultant. His publications include three books in Portuguese as well as *Eucharist and Globalization: Redrawing the Borders of Eucharistic Hospitality*, published in 2013.

Carvalhaes responded to the initial question about entertainment and worship with a reflection on the distinction between "high" art and "low" art. This differentiation, he says, began with Enlightenment thinkers like Immanuel Kant:

> With this distinction also comes the distinction between art by itself and religion. We have also the dichotomy between art and religious art. Religious people, especially in seminaries or churches, are afraid of art. On the other hand, what we have today with our universities is still this distinction. Many art theorists are allergic to religion. In some ways, because the way the field is structured, this is with good reason. Art wants to have this place of freedom to think, and religion has boundaries that limits the freedom of the artist. While art critics see religion as an impediment to art, religious people look at art as something that will mess up or disrespect their faith, their symbols, and their space.[44]

Worship, meanwhile, exhibits a similar dichotomy in which some traditions believe that liturgy is a God-sent event that must be done exactly as received, while other traditions do whatever they want. Carvalhaes sees dangers in both of these approaches, with authoritarian patriarchy on one side and cultural narcissism on the other. For him, there needs to be a transformative mixture, and the arts are a necessary part of that transformation.

Like Marcia McFee, Carvalhaes believes that there is much misunderstanding about the arts and performance in the church. People often think that performance is simply something that is done without any commitment to anything. However, even without their noticing, every play, show, dance, song, or any other entertainment changes them:

> Like worship, entertainment will transform you in some way or another because there is something that happens to you there. In that sense, performance is not "whatever." There is a deep commitment

---

44. Carvalhaes, interview, 2015.

for those who perform, there is hard work and conscious efforts to accomplish something. So this dichotomy between performance and worship is not helpful, for it makes us think that performance has no value and worship is not performance. If you understand worship, art for that matter, with this sense then we are all creating something, investing ourselves to put this "thing" together, because we all believe in it. Some people will call this thing, liturgy, holy or offensive, depending where they are, as also people will call any other cultural artistic performance, powerful, holy or offensive in the same way. I believe we must get beyond this sense of performance as something that is only secular, empty, not holy. We are all enacting something. Artists and religious people are putting a lot of love and work and gifts to these performances. And a lot of courage. Performance or entertainment then has to be understood in the same way as liturgy, even they have so many differences, complexities, and specificities.[45]

In the field of performance theory, worship itself is understood as performance, which includes the possibility of fun and enjoyment. As Carvalhaes points out, the performance of spirituality is often somber, quiet, with eyes closed or focused downward. He is somewhat sarcastic in his description of such events:

The creation of the sacred is also, not only, bound to cultural forms of understandings. You want to do something sacred in our culture? Light a candle and have everybody in silence. Oh, that is sacred! You don't speak, you don't talk, you don't move your body. That is how you do it. We have understood the Eucharist in that way, too, because there is death. This is so interesting because that sometimes doesn't even reflect the theologies of some churches. Nonetheless, you have to be quiet and go with this somber feeling to the table so you are respectful to God and fully spiritual. There is no possibility of celebrating the Resurrection as well with a joyful noise, dancing, clapping going around the table/altar. Thus, when we have only this sense of spirituality, anything that is fun or joyful sounds like an offense. That is why the performance of spirituality is seen as detached from the world or from the body, or any form of pleasure. We need to restore this joyful noise in the Christian spirituality.[46]

45. Carvalhaes, interview, 2015.
46. Carvalhaes, interview, 2015.

This sense of joy and celebration is enshrined in the first question of the Westminster Catechism, which declares that the purpose of humankind is to enjoy God forever. Unfortunately, says Carvalhaes, too often this sense of enjoyment gets lost in the worship customs of the church. Carvalhaes thinks it is necessary to expand the sense of performance and not see it as an enemy. Rather than performance being "against" worship, worship is a way of performing the presence of God, of learning to enjoy God. This is what he teaches his students as he encourages them to try new things:

> You are free. God wants us to be free! Try! Try, because not everything is going to work. That is the power of the community of all believers! Let's read our situation and try something together and figure out what it means. Failure is also a fundamental part of the creation and the doing of the worship, because this is not something somebody does on our behalf but we are doing it together. If it doesn't work, we don't do it again. That is how we build community too.[47]

When Carvalhaes was asked what it means to say that a ritual or an artwork works or does not work, he replied:

> When you say what works, we are talking about a series of things. The theological statements of that community; the ethical understandings of that community; the engagement with that community with a larger sense of community; the limits and possibilities of the people in that community. Everything has to be understood locally, not with universal criteria that might not work for every context. I think what works has to do with what that community is doing, what that community needs to be exposed to and needs to be kept from, what it needs to be engaging with. What works must be found together, experimenting, learning about it, seeing why this or that works or not, not simply dismissing it. The theology and the ethics of what works must always keep a door open to what is not known or controlled. That, I think, is the way to start to think about what works.[48]

In this understanding of worship, every worship service is destined to be a failure:

47. Carvalhaes, interview, 2015.

48. Carvalhaes, interview, 2015.

We cannot do the perfect worship. We cannot. As much as we try, there is no proper way of worshiping God. We are always falling behind.[49]

Nevertheless, it is important to keep trying, to keep rehearsing the ancient story and inviting the artists in to play with it. Because Carvalhaes is, himself, a performing artist, he has a lot of faith in what artists can bring to the church. He has an even greater faith in God, who loves us so much that we can try different things, even bringing artists into the church:

> A mature faith can deal with difference. Only the faith that is fearful cannot deal with difference and fences itself in fear and self-righteousness. That is why we often cannot deal with art because at makes us go places we shouldn't go and we can't control ourselves. So my fear with art is the same fear of the immigrant, the poor, the one from another tradition. We fence them away from us so we will feel safe. But the more we lock ourselves in a faith that cannot breathe the more violent and fearful we become. If my faith is grounded in a God that loves us all I am not afraid of anyone. I do not necessarily need to say yes to everything, but I don't need to enclose myself in a certain piety and/or hermetic beliefs. If God made me free, I can receive the immigrant, the artist and see them as gifts from the Holy Spirit to me and my community and not a threat.[50]

In this sense of freedom, the artists, liturgists, and theologians can listen for what the people need in each new moment:

> Definitely there will be other questions as old questions will persist. The plurality of our two thousand years of traditions gives us a wealth of possibilities, both to hold on to old practices as to create new practices for our times. In this way the questions are related to us. We are both going to be the same and are going to be very new because of the new ways of understanding the past and ourselves. Our time is pressing us to consider differences as gifts. Artists have this power to help us see the present and the future in new ways! They will both haunt and bless our spaces with criticism of our times and possibilities for it. Artists are immense gifts to our hearts, souls, and bodies. In many ways artists are always ahead with questions that we can't even ask. Our task is to catch up with them! And see how the ancient and the new can live together.

49. Carvalhaes, interview, 2015.
50. Carvalhaes, interview, 2015.

Look at what environmental artists are doing! Look at Daniel Beltran, Subhankar Banerjee, Paul Nicklen and Cristina Mittermeier, David Buckland, Basia Irland and many others. Or artists dealing with border such as Guillermo Gomez-Pena, ERRE, DoEAT and Margarita Garcia Asperas, Judi Werthein, Ana Teresa Fernandez. Or Doris Salcado, Tania Bruguera and many others. They are doing the work we are not doing. We desperately need them to deal with our reality and the questions that arise that our traditions have not been able to answer. In this way, I hope we will be able to expand our vision and see the ways in which our situation, the context of the economic, social, culture, racial, sexual, and historical context in which we are now, which affects our communities and how we can collectively engage our reality in most expansive and deeper ways for transformation.[51]

In the future of worship envisioned by Carvalhaes, there will always be room for celebration, for the arts, and for the Holy Spirit.

Where Do We Go From Here?

Everyone who lives in the borderland of entertainment, performance, art, and worship sees it from a different perspective. Clearly it is a struggle to articulate in words what the differences and similarities are, even as there seem to be many directions and possibilities. In looking for clear boundaries, it is easy to get tangled up in ambiguities and contradictions. The final chapter will look for patterns and try to offer some tentative conclusions.

51. Carvalhaes, interview, 2015.

seven

Performing the Gospel

The fire has its flame and praises God.
The wind blows the flame and praises God.
In the voice we hear the word which praises God.
And the word, when heard, praises God.
So all of creation is a song of praise to God.[1]

THIS STUDY BEGAN WITH a question about the relationship between good
entertainment and good worship, and the perception that sometimes what
is intended to be a service of Christian worship can seem no different than
a concert or a play, while what seems at the outset to be merely an entertainment can sometimes result in a profoundly spiritual experience. The
observation that some church services are perceived as boring, while others are accused of being overly entertaining, raised questions about how
performance and aesthetic issues are understood both within the church
and in society at large. Intended as more descriptive than normative, this
volume has noted how the performing arts can become contentious in
the context of Christian worship, and how the forms of Christian worship
sometimes slip into the rules and expectations of secular performance.

1. Hildegard of Bingen, as quoted in Fox, *Original Blessing*, 69.

A Blurry Tradition

As the opinions and examples in this volume have shown, wherever one tries to draw the line, it becomes more difficult to discern the closer one gets to it. This is not simply a modern concern. The earliest Christian worship seemed to be around dinner tables, where the host or elder would simply tell the Gospel story to the best of his or her ability or read one of the letters from Paul or another apostle, in the context of whatever table blessings were customary in that time and place. Since Paul castigates the Corinthians for their unchristian behavior at some of these gatherings, it is clear that at least some of those who attended did so more for the entertainment of eating and drinking together than for the purpose of praying and celebrating Christ's supper as one body.[2]

Partially as a result of Paul's chastisement, and partially because humans tend to make rules around what they do regularly in groups, over time these gatherings became more formalized, as is reflected in the earliest liturgical documents. Still, what some intended as worship others experienced as entertainment. Many people in Augustine's time came to hear the famous preacher because they were interested in spectacle rather than religious instruction or worship. Similarly, in the Middle Ages, preachers were as much a source of entertainment as edification, and many in the leisured classes, at least, attended Mass more as a form of diversion than out of real devotion.

In more recent periods, the nineteenth-century revivalists like Charles Finney, the charismatic preachers of the mid- to late-twentieth century like Billy Graham and Robert Schuller, and today's televangelists and leaders of mega-churches continue to blur the line between worship and entertainment. While some might accuse them of being too slick, too practiced, or even cynical hypocrites preying on the weakness of their devoted followers, others cannot get enough of their inspirational messages and well-practiced performance of Christian worship.

Exploring the Borderlands

In exploring these borderlands where worship, entertainment, and the arts meet, it is easy to get lost among the particulars. At first, there seem to be bright, clear boundaries between Christian worship and entertainment,

2. See 1 Cor 11:17–34.

as well as between entertainment and art. Christian worship is marked, as Gail Ramshaw says so eloquently, by "the ritual through which the baptized community renders prayer and praise to God." Likewise, both Gordon Lathrop and Tom Long distinguish between congregations, which gather for the purpose of Christian worship and are marked by their baptismal identity, and audiences, who gather as individuals for their pleasure in being entertained.

Most of the others who have served as guides through this confusing terrain have been less willing to point to lines than to indicate where the boundaries have been blurred or even erased, or to raise other issues that further complicate the conversation. For instance, Kim Harris refuses to differentiate at all between worship and entertainment, even as she notes the differing expectations of her as a performer when she brings the same songs to a church service, a folk concert, or even a classroom.

Similarly, Tracy Radosevic and Carl Petter Opsahl do not distinguish between audiences and congregations, speaking of both interchangeably. Radosevic, especially, makes the point that worship is, or should be, entertaining, and sees no problem with that characterization. Opsahl, in his ministry to street people and prisoners, is eager that whatever else happens, those who are present should at least have a good time.

Janet Walton, whose influence as a teacher can be seen in the thought of Harris, Opsahl, Cláudio Carvalhaes, and others who did their doctoral work with her, makes a slightly different point. Rather than asking whether some given activity is worship or entertainment, she is concerned with the effect of that activity on the community. For her, if the more entertaining aspects of worship wake people up, make them more receptive, move them to action, or simply make them smile, that is a good thing.

Others, like Lisa Cole Smith and Mark Miller, take a wider definition of worship than simply what Christians do when they gather. Smith encourages her congregation to see the whole of life as worship, with the intentional gathering for that purpose in a communal way as simply one expression of that worshipful life. Miller would probably agree, while wanting worship to be as playful, full of life, and whimsical as good entertainment.

Marcia McFee does note the distinction but, like Marlita Hill, is more concerned with the notions surrounding performance than defining whether something that happens in a worship service might or might not be entertainment. Both McFee and Hill want people in the church to understand performance not as something that is presented for others to appreciate, but as a skilled and thoughtful way to help others engage with God. Tom Long is similarly concerned with performance issues, noting that a preacher giving the same sermon for the third time on a particular Sunday needs to draw on the same kind of preparation and integrity as an actor in a long run to make the Word present, alive, and authentic for the congregation.

Engagement is also an important concern for Roy Barber. Like Miller, Barber believes that both theater and worship are opportunities to engage people, to draw them into a moment of encounter with themselves and with God. Heather Josselyn-Cranson struggles with a different aspect of engagement, asking how congregations can be encouraged to listen in an active way, rather than sitting back and expecting those who are leading to worship on their behalf.

Several people grappled with the idea of excellence in worship, noting that this can mean different things to different people. Eileen Guenther stresses that excellence comes from preparation, and while the Holy Spirit can override mistakes, it is important to strive for excellence for the good of the entire worshipping body. Likewise, Ruth Duck grounds excellence in love and care, while pointing out that the more highly trained participants are there to bring out the gifts of the congregation. Meanwhile, Geoffrey Moore grounds excellence in intentionality and narrative, which together help both audiences and congregations understand what is happening and why.

Narrative is central for Melva Sampson and Ken Fong, also. Sampson likens the performance of preaching to telling stories at family gatherings, holding up the ancestral memories in the musicality of the oral tradition. Fong, on the other hand, sees similarities between preaching and stand-up comedy, while cautioning that humor alone is insufficient in helping people hear from God through the earthen vessel of the preacher.

For Don Saliers, from whom the concept of "borderland" in this volume is borrowed, the line between entertainment and worship has no fixed position, but rather is a matter of context, shifting and changing according to who is present and what other events are influencing the experience. Similarly, Heather Murray Elkins intentionally blurs the line for her students, inviting performing artists to think of what they do as proclamation, and preachers to understand their task as performance.

Finally, Cláudio Carvalhaes challenges his students to reconsider their ideas about performance, art, and worship, noting that good entertainment takes the same kind of commitment and integrity that is needed for good worship. Like Mark Miller, Carvalhaes wants to restore a sense of joy, celebration, and wonder to worship that, too often, is so somber and serious that no one feels free to move their body or even to smile or laugh. While neither wants to ignore tradition, Christian worship is an opportunity to experiment, to try things out, as well as to be mindful of tradition. After all, we never get it completely right. As Annie Dillard puts it, "Week after week Christ washes the disciples' dirty feet, handles their very toes, and repeats, It is all right—believe it or not—to be people. Who can believe it?"[3]

Patterns and Guideposts

In summarizing these responses, several things stand out. In general, people who have similar backgrounds tend to come to the questions from similar directions. Thus, the dancers talked about performance, preachers talked about narrative, musicians talked about excellence, and actors preferred to find commonalities rather than distinctions. There were, naturally, many exceptions and a great deal of nuance in what individuals bring to the conversation. Perhaps the most important pattern was the genuine passion and concern that characterized each interview, as each person tried to find adequate words to distinguish between performance and authenticity, between putting on an act and bringing one's best, between entertainment and art, and how all of these relate to worshiping God together as a congregation.

As my guides and colleagues showed me their favorite paths through the borderlands of worship, entertainment, and the arts, I repeatedly found myself in places that felt both familiar and filled with new possibilities. Whenever I thought it might be possible to draw a clear, bright line between worship and entertainment, between entertainment and art, between performance and authenticity, the landscape shifted, revealing nuances and vistas that I had not previously seen. This is true not only when looking at the opinions and experiences of those who are writing, thinking, and planning worship today, but also in the long historical record of Christian worship.

Egeria's excitement at taking part in the processions and prayers in fifth-century Jerusalem was both genuine worship and a kind of playacting. To ask whether this was worship or entertainment, ritual or art, is to ask the wrong questions. Those who organized the events that Egeria

3. Dillard, "Expedition to the Pole," 38.

recounts embellished the natural theatricality of the biblical geography with luxurious fabrics, candlelit processions, and other artificial devices to draw the pilgrims into a heightened state in which they could feel as if they were part of the crowd who followed Jesus to hear him preach on the Mount of Olives, see him raise Lazarus from the dead in Bethany, or hear his last words on the cross at Golgotha. As Egeria and her fellow pilgrims followed what became known as the Via Dolorosa, many of them not only identified with Jesus during his passion and death, but also came into a more profound relationship with God that remained with them even after they returned to their homes.

Centuries later, the Benedictines who were sitting in quire on Easter morning, hearing the astonishingly beautiful music of the angels who asked the women who they were looking for, must have felt at least a little like being in heaven, eternally witnessing the presence of the risen Christ. Likewise, the people who thronged the streets of York to watch members of the various guilds play God and Satan at the beginning of time or Adam and Eve eat from the tree of knowledge, were both having a rousing good time and being reminded that they, too, were integral parts of the sacred mystery that the plays depicted.

The stories of Egeria, mystery plays, revival meetings, royal weddings, and clown communions can serve as both guideposts and cautionary tales for those who are exploring the shifting landscape of worship. Here are a few of the signs that can help those who plan, lead, and think about good worship know that they are on the right path:

- The primary difference between Christian worship and entertainment is the intention that people bring to it. While audiences may have a transcendent experience at a concert, play, or Broadway show, an audience is not a congregation, and people do not go to a comedy club in order to worship God. Nevertheless, those who plan worship not only can, but often should, include elements that are entertaining, that open those who attend to the presence of the Holy Spirit, that make people smile or even laugh out loud.

- Whether teaching a roomful of students who would rather be anywhere else, preaching the same sermon for the third time, or leading a worship service after a sleepless night, it is necessary to draw on the same kind of skills and energy that actors use to wake up a sleepy crowd while being both fully themselves and fully the character that they are to embody. In thinking about what it means to perform the Gospel, the goal is always to be as authentic, embodied, and true as possible while simultaneously being fully present to the movements of the Holy Spirit among and through the gathered body.

- Everything that happens in a worship service should be appropriate to the day and place. Just as sawdust on the floor might be expected at the circus but not at the concert hall, the high formality of worship that is appropriate at the National Cathedral might seem pretentious in a small, rural congregation. Conversely, the homespun familiarity of worship at the proverbial Saint Joe's by the Gas Station, where worshipers show up in overalls or shorts, might be out of place at a church where everyone always wears their Sunday best.

- Thoughtful planning, in which everyone is both literally and figuratively on the same page, is a sign of excellence. When the subject matter keeps changing, the congregation gets confused and disengages. As in a good play or movie, good worship depends on thematic unity, a through-line that holds the service together with a discernible beginning, middle, and end. Scripture readings, hymns, sermons, prayers, and other elements that reflect or comment on one another help the congregation move more deeply into communion with God, with one another, and with the world.

- No worship service is ever perfect. Knowing that allows for the freedom to experiment, to improvise, to try different ways of helping the congregation learn to celebrate the presence of God. If something doesn't work this week, then try something else next time.

These, of course, are only suggestions, reminders that how the landscape looks depends on where you stand.

Wherever Two or Three Are Gathered

It is not possible, or even desirable, for those whose professional lives are devoted to what happens in Christian worship to have any control over that part of the borderland that is clearly labeled entertainment. Even the ambiguous terrain that includes concerts consisting of sacred music, plays that bring audiences into an awareness of the divine, or entertainment figures like Chance the Rapper making an altar call in the midst of a concert cannot rightly be considered as gatherings of the baptized, assembling for the purpose of praise and prayer.

However, legitimate questions can be raised about sound-and-light shows that take place inside cathedrals; weddings that are at least as much spectacle as Christian sacrament; and popular songs that replace music with explicitly Christian lyrics in a worship service. When ordained persons dress as clowns to preside at communion, a priest merrily twirls down the aisle instead of processing in a stately manner, or an organist plays themes from popular films at the offertory, are they illegitimately conflating entertainment with worship, or are they drawing people into the presence of God? Is using the Sunday morning congregational gathering for a performance of Handel's *Messiah*, a production of *Murder in the Cathedral*, or the contemplation of paintings by a member of the congregation, a legitimate way to worship God, or do such activities shade into the worship of art? Is dramatizing Bible stories, hiring professional singers for the choir, or borrowing the techniques of stand-up comedy to enliven the sermon crossing a line, or simply making worship more relevant and less boring?

Perhaps the most important conclusion that one can draw from this study is that there is no consensus when it comes to performing the Gospel. What one person sees as clearly over the line, another believes is not only permissible but an important way of carrying the tradition into the present moment. What one person experiences as a distraction from the prayers and praise of God, another finds deeply meaningful and important not only for their own spiritual development, but for that of the community. The rituals, songs, and preaching styles that are life-giving and soul-satisfying to some are empty, repetitive, clanging gongs to others.

There probably is no single answer to these difficult questions that can satisfy everyone. There is probably no approach to worship that everyone will find equally nourishing. There is probably no line in the borderlands that everyone will see equally clearly. There is no one, single way to perform the Gospel that can reach everyone. That is probably a good thing, as God is bigger than all of us and all that we can imagine. In the end, the Gospel will be performed wherever two or three are gathered together, listening for the Word of God, feeling the breath of the Spirit dancing in and among and through them, feeding one another so that they can become what they already are: members of the Body of Christ, going out to perform the Good News of God's love for the healing of the world.

Bibliography

Applebaum, David. "Focus." *Parabola: Myth, Tradition, and the Search for Meaning* 21 (1996) 1.

Augustine. *Confessions.* Translated by Edward Bouverie Pousey. Oxford: John Henry Parker, 1840. Kindle.

————. *On Christian Doctrine.* Translated by Edward Bouverie Pousey. London: Encyclopaedia Britannica, 1952. http://faculty.georgetown.edu/jod/augustine/ddc4. html.

Basilique Notre-Dame de Montreal. "Masses and Adoration" (2018). https://www. basiliquenotredame.ca/en/messes-et-adoration.

Bell, Catherine M. *Ritual Theory, Ritual Practice.* New York: Oxford University Press, 2009.

Booth, William, and Karla Adam. "At Prince Harry and Meghan Markle's Royal Wedding, Some Things Very Old and Some Things New." *Washington Post,* May 20, 2018.

Brown, Frank Burch. *Good Taste, Bad Taste, and Christian Taste: Aesthetics in Religious Life.* Oxford: Oxford University Press, 2003.

Burkhart, John E. *Worship: A Searching Examination of the Liturgical Experience.* Philadelphia: Westminster John Knox, 1982.

Cargill, Oscar. *Drama and Liturgy.* New York: Octagon Books by special arrangement with Columbia University Press, 1930.

Carroll, Lewis. *Through the Looking Glass and What Alice Found There.* Philadelphia: Henry Altemus, 1897.

Childers, Jana. *Performing the Word: Preaching as Theatre.* Nashville: Abingdon, 1998.

Childers, Jana, and Clayton F. Schmit, eds. *Performance in Preaching: Bringing the Sermon to Life.* Grand Rapids: Baker Academic, 2008.

Clement of Alexandria. *The Instructor,* Book III. http://www.newadvent.org/fathers/02093. htm.

Congregational Library and Archive. "Puritans and Entertainment." *Beacon Street Diary Blog,* August 9, 2012. http://www.congregationallibrary.org/blog/201208/puritans-and-entertainment.

Cotton, Dean. "Don't Neglect Sharing Our Gifts." *World Clown Association Clown Ministry Insights* 2018. https://www.worldclown.com/clown-ministry-insights.html.

Council of Trent. "On Preachers of the Word of God, and on Questors of Alms." In *Session V: On Reformation.* http://www.thecounciloftrent.com/ch5.htm.

Dewey, Dennis. "That's Entertainment?" https://sacredstoryjourneys.files.wordpress. com/2016/01/thats-entertainment.pdf.

Dillard, Annie. "An Expedition to the Pole." In *Teaching a Stone to Talk: Expeditions and Encounters*. New York: Harper Colophon, 1983.

Driver, Tom F. *Liberating Rites: Understanding the Transformative Power of Ritual*. Boulder: Westview, 1997.

Duffy, Eamon. *The Stripping of the Altars*. New Haven: Yale University Press, 1992.

Dunsch, Boris. "Religion in Roman Comedy." In *The Oxford Handbook of Greek and Roman Comedy*. Oxford Handbooks, 2014. http://www.oxfordhandbooks.com/view/10.1093/oxfordhb/9780199743544.001.0001/oxfordhb-9780199743544-e-032.

Egeria. *Egeria: Diary of a Pilgrimage*. Translated by George E. Gingras. New York: Newman, 1970.

Elkins, James. *Why Art Cannot Be Taught: A Handbook for Art Students*. Urbana: University of Illinois Press, 2001.

Eyes to See, Ears to Hear, Peace Prayer Mission Group. "Guns: From Despair to Hope," December 13, 2015. http://www.seekerschurch.org/gun-violence-despair-to-hope-by-the-eyes-to-see-ears-to-hear-peace-prayer-mission-group/.

"Finding God at a Beyoncé Mass." YouTube, 2018. https://www.youtube.com/watch?v=PXci-sRayAQ.

Fox, Matthew. *Original Blessing*. Santa Fe: Bear, 1983.

Geurts, Kathryn. *Culture and the Senses: Bodily Ways of Knowing in an African Community*. Berkeley: University of California Press, 2003.

Gilbert, Marlea, Christopher Grundy, Eric T. Myers, and Stephanie Perdew. *The Work of the People: What We Do in Worship and Why*. Vital Worship, Healthy Congregations. Herndon, VA: Rowman & Littlefield Publishers, 2006.

Grace Cathedral. "The Vine." 2018. https://www.gracecathedral.org/thevine/.

Grainger, Roger. *The Drama of the Rite: Worship, Liturgy and Theatre Performance*. Brighton, UK: Sussex Academic Press, 2009.

Hardison, O. B. *Christian Rite and Christian Drama in the Middle Ages: Essays in the Origin and Early History of Modern Drama*. Westport, CT: Greenwood, 1983.

Harmon, Katherine E. "The Legitimate Liturgical Function of Clowns." *Pray Tell: Worship, Wit & Wisdom*, 2014. http://www.praytellblog.com/index.php/2014/09/29/the-legitimate-liturgical-function-of-clowns/.

Harvey, Kerric. "Interrogation Project Flyer," 2016.

Hippolytus. *The Apostolic Tradition*. Translated by Burton Scott Easton. Cambridge: Cambridge University Press, 1934.

Hornaday, Anne. "What Defines a 'Must-See' Movie? And Does 'Infinity War' Make the Cut?" *Washington Post*, May 11, 2018. https://www.washingtonpost.com/lifestyle/style/what-defines-a-must-see-movie-and-does-infinity-war-make-the-cut/2018/05/10/0dd923ec-5457-11e8-9c91-7dab596e8252_story.html?noredirect=on&utm_term=.6153e8d6e403.

Hudson, Anne. "The Sermons of Ms Longleat 4." *Medium Aevum* 53 (1984) 220–38.

Huizinga, Johan. "What 'Play' Is: Engagement and Absorption." *Parabola: Myth, Tradition, and the Search for Meaning* XXI (1996) 59–63.

Johnson, David Brent. "Sacred Blue: Jazz Goes to the Church in the 1960s." *Night Lights: Classic Jazz*, 2011. https://indianapublicmedia.org/nightlights/sacred-blue-jazz-church-1960s/.

Johnson, Todd Eric, and Dale Savidge, eds. *Performing the Sacred: Theology and Theatre in Dialogue*. Grand Rapids: Baker Academic, 2009.

Johnson, Trygve David. *The Preacher as Liturgical Artist: Metaphor, Identity, and the Vicarious Humanity of Christ*. Eugene, OR: Cascade, 2014.

Kavanagh, Aidan. *Elements of Rite: A Handbook of Liturgical Style*. New York: Pueblo, 1982.

Kierkegaard, Søren. *Purity of Heart Is to Will One Thing: Spiritual Preparation for the Office of Confession*. Translated by Douglas V. Steeres. New York: Harper, 1956.

Kivy, Peter. *Authenticities: Philosophical Reflections on Musical Performance*. Ithaca: Cornell University Press, 1997.

Kristeller, Paul Oskar. *Renaissance Thought II: Papers on Humanism and the Arts*. New York: Harper & Row, 1965.

Larsen, Josh. *Movies Are Prayers: How Films Voice Our Deepest Longings*. Downers Grove, IL: InterVarsity, 2017.

LaRue, Cleophus J. *I Believe I'll Testify: The Art of African American Preaching*. Louisville: Westminster John Knox, 2011.

LaRue, Donna. "Tripudium: Its Use in Sources From 200 BCE to 1600 CE." *ARTS: Arts in Religious and Theological Studies* 7 (1995) 25–29.

Libaw, Oliver. "More Americans Flock to Mega-Churches." *ABC News*, 2014. http://abcnews.go.com/US/story?id=93111.

McCall, Richard D. *Do This: Liturgy as Performance*. Notre Dame: University of Notre Dame Press, 2007.

Moment Factory website. "About." *Moment Factory*, 2018. https://momentfactory.com/about.

"Montreal's Notre-Dame Basilica Hosts Stunning Light Shows that Are Pure Magic." *Facebook*, 2018. https://www.facebook.com/OMGFacts/videos/vb.231435026494/1834712036831295/?type=2&theater.

Mosby, Karen E. "'I Speak to God in Public': The Black Millennial Theology and Activism of Chance the Rapper." Paper presented at the Biennial Conference of the Association of Practical Theology, New Haven, CT, April, 2018.

MTO Staff. "Episcopal Church Holds a 'Worship Beyoncé' Mass. Said Special 'Beyoncé' Prayers." *MTO News*, 2018. https://mtonews.com/episcopal-church-holds-a-worship-beyonce-mass-said-special-beyonce-prayers.

Muir, Edward. *Ritual in Early Modern Europe*. Cambridge: Cambridge University Press, 1997.

Paulsell, Stephanie. "Writing as a Spiritual Discipline." In *The Scope of Our Art: The Vocation of the Theological Teacher*, edited by Gregory L. Jones and Stephanie Paulsell, 17–31. Grand Rapids: Eerdmans, 2001.

Postman, Neil. *Amusing Ourselves to Death: Public Discourse in the Age of Show Business*. New York: Viking, 1985.

Radcliffe, Timothy. *Why Go to Church?: The Drama of the Eucharist*. London: Bloomsbury Academic, 2009.

Rock, Judith, and Norman Mealy. *Performer as Priest and Prophet: Restoring the Intuitive in Worship Through Music and Dance*. San Francisco: Harper and Row, 1988.

Rue, Victoria. *Acting Religious: Theatre as Pedagogy in Religious Studies*. Cleveland: Pilgrim, 2005.

Saliers, Don, and Emily Saliers. *A Song to Sing, a Life to Live: Reflections on Music as Spiritual Practice*. San Francisco: Jossey-Bass, 2006.

Schechner, Richard. *Essays on Performance Theory, 1970-1976*. New York: Drama Book Specialists, 1977.

Second Vatican Council. *Sacrosanctum Concilium* [Constitution of the Sacred Liturgy]. 1963. http://www.vatican.va/archive/hist_councils/ii_vatican_council/documents/vat-ii_const_19631204_sacrosanctum-concilium_en.html.

Seligman, Adam B., Robert P. Weller, Michael J. Puett, and Bennettt Simon. *Ritual and Its Consequences: An Essay on the Limits of Sincerity*. Oxford: Oxford University Press, 2008.

Taylor, W. David O., ed. *For the Beauty of the Church: Casting a Vision for the Arts*. Grand Rapids: Baker, 2010.

Westmoreland Festival Chorus. "Light in Deepest Night." Concert program, Westmoreland Congregational United Church of Christ, Bethesda, MD, December 12, 2015.

White, James F. *A Brief History of Christian Worship*. Nashville: Abingdon, 1993.

Wilson-Kastner, Patricia. *Sacred Drama: A Spirituality of Christian Liturgy*. Minneapolis: Fortress, 1999.

Wolterstorff, Nicholas. *Art Rethought: The Social Practices of Art*. Oxford: Oxford University Press, 2017.

Yarnold, Edward. *The Awe-Inspiring Rites of Initiation: Baptismal Homilies of the Fourth Century*. Slough, UK: St Paul Publications, 1972.

Young, Malcom Clemens. "About the Beyoncé Mass." Grace Cathedral, 2018. https://www.gracecathedral.org/about-the-beyonce-mass/.

Zauzmer, Julie. "A New Spin on Loaves and Fishes." *Washington Post*, March 5, 2018.

Interviews

Barber, Roy. Interview by author. Video recording. Washington, DC, October 12, 2015.

Carvalhaes, Cláudio. Interview by author. Video recording. Atlanta, November 22, 2015.

Duck, Ruth. Interview by author. Video recording. Chicago, January 15, 2016.

Elkins, Heather Murray. Interview by author. Video recording. Houston, January 9, 2017.

Fong, Ken. Interview by author. Audio recording. Los Angeles, November 4, 2015.

Guenther, Eileen. Interview by author. Video recording. Washington, DC, February 1, 2016.

Harris, Kim. Interview by author. Audio recording. Los Angeles, August 14, 2015.

Hill, Marlita. Interview by author. Audio recording. Los Angeles, July 24, 2015.

Josselyn-Cranson, Heather. Interview by author. Video recording. Houston, January 8, 2016.

Lathrop, Gordon. Interview by author. Video recording. Washington, DC, November 30, 2015.

Long, Thomas G. Interview by author. Video recording. Atlanta, November 22, 2015.

McFee, Marcia. Interview by author. Video recording. Truckee, CA, July 27, 2015.

Miller, Mark. Interview by author. Video recording. Houston, January 8, 2016.

Moore, Geoffrey. Interview by author. Video recording. Houston, January 8, 2016.

Opsahl, Carl Petter. Interview by author. Video recording. Houston, January 10, 2016.

Radosevic, Tracy. Interview by author. Video recording. Washington, DC, September 29, 2015.

Ramshaw, Gail. Letter to author. Washington, April 29, 2015.

Saliers, Don. Interview by author. Video recording. Houston, January 8, 2016.

Sampson, Melva. Interview by author. Video recording. Atlanta, January 5, 2016.

Smith, Lisa Cole. Interview by author. Video recording. Washington, DC, October 23, 2015.

Walton, Janet. Interview by author. Video recording. Houston, January 9, 2016.

Appendix

About the Experts

OVER THE COURSE OF the past three years, twenty-one artists, scholars, and liturgical experts gave generously of their time, energy, and knowledge. The brief biographies below, listed this time in alphabetical order by last name, recapitulate the information about each of them that is already in the text, adding pointers to websites, videos, books, and other resources. While web links are always subject to change, at the time of this writing, all of them were live.

Roy Barber

Roy Barber is a musician, playwright, and teacher. He works with the Bokamoso Youth Center, a nonprofit organization in Winterveldt township in South Africa. Bokamoso helps young people at risk learn to be contributing members of society and finish their schooling. For a number of years, Barber has helped a group of singers, dancers, and actors from Bokamoso come to the US every January to perform a musical based on stories drawn from their own lives and to acquire skills that will help them find meaningful work when they return to their homes.

I interviewed Barber in my office in Washington, DC, on October 12, 2015, and recorded the conversation on video. More about Roy Barber may be found on the website of StreetSense Media at https://www.streetsense-media.org/staff_members/roy-barber/#.WzbONqkh1oc. Barber serves as artist-in-residence at Street Sense, an organization of people experiencing homelessness, and is one of the volunteer leaders of Staging Hope, a weekly workshop on playwriting and staged performance that is offered to Street Sense members.

Cláudio Carvalhaes

Cláudio Carvalhaes is associate professor of worship at Union Theological Seminary in New York, an ordained teaching elder in the Presbyterian Church (USA), and a much-sought-after speaker, writer, performer, and consultant. His publications include three books in Portuguese as well as *Eucharist and Globalization: Redrawing the Borders of Eucharistic Hospitality,* published in 2013.

I interviewed Carvalhaes on the exhibitions floor of the annual meeting of the American Academy of Religion/Society of Biblical Literature in Atlanta on November 22, 2015, and recorded the conversation on video. More about Cláudio Carvalhaes may be found on his faculty page at Union Theological Seminary at https://utsnyc.edu/faculty/claudio-carvalhaes/ and his own website at http://www.claudiocarvalhaes.com/.

Ruth Duck

Ruth Duck recently retired as professor of worship at Garrett-Evangelical Theological Seminary, where she was on the faculty since 1989. She was president of the North American Academy of Liturgy, an organization of liturgical scholars, in 2007. She has written many books and articles about Christian worship, as well as numerous hymn texts that are found in the various denominational hymnals. Her 2013 book, *Worship for the Whole People of God: Vital Worship for the 21st Century,* is widely used as a text in courses on worship.

I interviewed Duck online while she was in Chicago and I was in Washington, DC, on January 15, 2016, and recorded the conversation on video. More about Ruth Duck may be found at her website: https://ruthduckhymnist.net/.

Heather Murray Elkins

Heather Murray Elkins is professor of worship, preaching, and the arts at the Theological School of Drew University in Madison, New Jersey, and an ordained elder in the West Virginia Annual Conference of the United Methodist Church. Her courses include sacramental preaching, worship, narrative theology, ritual, and Appalachian studies.

I interviewed Elkins at the annual meeting of the North American Academy of Liturgy in Houston on January 9, 2016, and recorded the conversation on video. Her Youtube series, *Holy Stuff of Life*, based on storytelling, object relations, and the Christian year, may be found at https://www.youtube.com/channel/UC3ff_PeRKKX4BoBq8EN_eJQ.

Ken Fong

Ken Fong is well-known in the Asian American Christian community as a courageous pastor, teacher, and thinker who is a leading progressive voice among American Baptists and other evangelicals. Fong recently retired after twenty-one years as the senior pastor of Evergreen Baptist Church of Los Angeles (now in Rosemead, California), a large pan-Asian, multi-ethnic congregation. He now serves as affiliate associate professor of Asian American church studies at Fuller Theological Seminary.

An audio recording was made of my telephone interview with Fong when he was in Los Angeles and I was in Washington, DC, on November 4, 2015. His weekly podcast, *Asian America*, may be found at http://asianamericapodcast.com/. Information about the forthcoming documentary about his calling to find a better way for openly LGBTQ folks and the evangelical church to come together is available at https://www.indiegogo.com/projects/the-ken-fong-project#/.

Eileen Guenther

Eileen Guenther is professor of church music at Wesley Theological Seminary, where she teaches music and worship courses and serves as director of chapel music. A church musician, teacher, scholar, and conductor, she is also three-term president of the American Guild of Organists. Her publications include *Rivals or a Team: Clergy-Musician Relationships in the Twenty-First Century* and *In Their Own Words: Slave Life and the Power of Spirituals*.

I interviewed Guenther in her office in Washington, DC, on February 1, 2016, and recorded the conversation on video. More about Eileen Guenther is available on her Wesley Theological Seminary faculty web page at https://www.wesleyseminary.edu/employees/eileen-guenther/ and on her own website at https://www.eileenguenther.com/.

Kim Harris

Kim Harris is professor of theological studies at Loyola University's Bellarmine College of Liberal Arts. She is also a musician who writes, records, and produces music as a means to promote creativity, education, social responsibility, and understanding in the world community. Her mass setting, *Welcome Table: A Mass of Spirituals*, sets the text of the newly revised *Third Edition of the Roman Missal* to the melodies of spirituals, using recognizable tunes in their totality to present an authentic rendering of the music in the context of the liturgy. Information about *Welcome Table* may be found at http://www.kimandreggie.com/kim_phd_ooo.htm.

An audio recording was made of my telephone interview with Harris when she was in Los Angeles and I was in Washington, DC, on August 14, 2015. More about Kim Harris is available on the Loyola Marymount University "Women of Color Oral History Project" at http://oralhistory.wgst1100borgia.lmu.build/raidy/.

Marlita Hill

Marlita Hill is the choreographer and artistic director of Speak Hill Dance Company, based in southern California. She is the author of *Defying Discord: Ending the Divide between Your Faith and "Secular" Art Career* and the book series *Dancers! Assume the Position*, produces a weekly podcast called *The Kingdom Art Life*, and is the creator of "The Kingdom Artist Initiative," a discipleship program for artists working in secular culture. She also serves as the associate director for Edge Project, an organization focused on art, culture, and faith.

An audio recording was made of my telephone interview with Hill when she was in Los Angeles and I was in Washington, DC, on July 24, 2015. More about Marlita Hill and her projects may be found on her website at http://marlitahill.com/.

Heather Josselyn-Cranson

Heather Josselyn-Cranson holds the Sister Margaret William McCarthy Endowed Chair in Music at Regis College, a Catholic university in greater Boston. Josselyn-Cranson teaches in the fields of music and religion, including classes on the New Testament, spiritual autobiographies, music and health, and ethnomusicology. She also directs the Regis Chamber Singers and the Regis Glee Singers. Her scholarship focuses on the intersection of music and worship, both in modern-day Emerging Church contexts as well as in the medieval monastic context of the Order of Sempringham.

I interviewed Josselyn-Cranson at the annual meeting of the North American Academy of Liturgy in Houston on January 9, 2016, and recorded the conversation on video. Read more about Heather Josselyn-Cranson on her faculty web page at Regis, https://www.regiscollege.edu/heather-josselyn-cranson.

Gordon Lathrop

Gordon W. Lathrop is professor of liturgy emeritus at the Lutheran Theological Seminary in Philadelphia. A pastor of the Evangelical Lutheran Church in America, he is the author of several books, has lectured widely in several countries, and has participated in the work of the Faith and Order Commission of the World Council of Churches and the Worship and Culture Study of the Lutheran World Federation.

I interviewed Lathrop in my office in Washington, DC, on November 30, 2015, and recorded the interview on video. His 2017 talk on "Reformation & Liturgical Reform: Ecumenical Perspectives" may be found at https://www.youtube.com/watch?v=CtGoxnbgCho.

Thomas G. Long

Tom Long is Bandy Professor Emeritus of Preaching and Director of the Early Career Pastoral Leadership Program at Emory University's Candler School of Theology. He is an ordained minister in the Presbyterian Church (USA), served as the senior homiletics editor of *The New Interpreter's Bible*, and is associate editor of *Journal for Preachers* and editor-at-large for *The Christian Century*.

I interviewed Long at the annual meeting of the American Academy of Religion in Atlanta on November 22, 2015, and recorded the conversation on video. More about Tom Long may be found on his Candler School of Theology faculty web page, http://candler.emory.edu/faculty/profiles/long-thomas.html.

Marcia McFee

Marcia McFee is an author, worship designer and leader, professor, preacher, and artist. Her engaging and interactive style has been called "refreshing," "inspiring," and "unforgettable." McFee combines her background and experience in professional companies of music, theater, and dance with a variety of worship and preaching styles in order to bring a fresh experience of the Gospel to each worship setting. She has provided worship design and leadership at numerous international and regional gatherings.

I interviewed McFee online when she was in Truckee and I was in Washington, DC, on July 27, 2015, and made a video recording of that conversation. More can be found about Marcia McFee on her website: http://marciamcfee.com/.

Mark Miller

Mark Miller serves as associate professor of church music at Drew Theological School and is a lecturer in the practice of sacred music at Yale University. He also is the minister of music at Christ Church in Summit, New Jersey. Since 1999 Miller has led music for United Methodists and others around the country, including directing music for the 2008 General Conference. His choral anthems are best sellers for Abingdon Press and Choristers Guild and his hymns are published in *Worship & Song, Sing! Prayer and Praise, Zion Still Sings, Amazing Abundance, The Faith We Sing*, and other hymnals.

I interviewed Miller at the annual meeting of the North American Academy of Liturgy in Houston on January 8, 2016. Read more about Mark Miller in the article "Sing Out!" on the Drew University website at http://www.drew.edu/news/2016/04/14/sing-out and his own website at http://www.markamillermusic.com/.

Geoffrey C. Moore

Geoffrey C. Moore is a PhD candidate at Southern Methodist University's Dedman College of Humanities and Science, where his work has focused on sacramental theology and on examining the intersection of music and theology. Moore serves as the president of the Hymn Society in the United States and Canada and is a commissioned elder in the North Texas Conference of the United Methodist Church.

I interviewed Moore at the annual meeting of the North American Academy of Liturgy in Houston on January 8, 2016, and recorded our conversation on video. More information about Geoffrey Moore may be found on his page at Dedman College of Humanities and Sciences, Southern Methodist University, https://www.smu.edu/Dedman/Academics/Departments/ReligiousStudies/Graduate/CurrentStudents/gmoore.

Carl Petter Opsahl

Carl Petter Opsahl is a Lutheran pastor, jazz musician, and journalist. In 2002–03 he was a visiting scholar at Union Theological Seminary in the City of New York, where he received his doctorate in theology in 2012 with a thesis on spirituality and hip-hop culture, "Dance to My Ministry: Exploring Hip-Hop Spirituality." His other publications include *En fortelling om jazz* (A tale of jazz,), and *En god dag. Fortellinger til inspirasjon og ettertanke* (A good day. Stories of inspiration and reflection) as well as several solo and collaborative albums.

I interviewed Opsahl at the annual meeting of the North American Academy of Liturgy in Houston on January 10, 2016, and recorded our conversation on video. A Wikipedia entry for Carl Petter Opsahl at https://en.wikipedia.org/wiki/Carl_Petter_Opsahl discusses his many musical accomplishments.

Tracy Radosevic

Tracy Radosevic is an adjunct instructor at Wesley Theological Seminary, where she teaches biblical storytelling. She is a dynamic, energetic, internationally acclaimed storyteller, educator, and retreat facilitator. Since 1991 she has traveled all over the United States, as well as to several foreign countries, bringing her special brand of humor, insight, and faith to audiences of all ages through the power of narrative.

I interviewed Radosevic in my office in Washington, DC, on September 29, 2015, recording our conversation on video. Her website, http://tracyrad.com/, includes more of her thoughts on biblical storytelling, a longer version of her biography, and information on her retreats, workshops, and performances.

Gail Ramshaw

Gail Ramshaw is a retired professor of religion who studies and crafts liturgical language from her home outside of Washington, DC. Her many publications include *Treasures Old and New: Images in the Lectionary* and *The Three-Day Feast: Maundy Thursday, Good Friday, and Easter*. She currently serves as an editorial consultant for the journals *Worship* and *Studia Liturgica*.

Ramshaw's brief letter to me regarding her thoughts on the relationship of worship and entertainment is dated April 29, 2015. A fuller understanding of Gail Ramshaw's thought may be found in her many books and articles, which have influenced the teaching and practice of liturgics for the past twenty-five years. More about Gail Ramshaw and her writing may be found on her Amazon author page at https://www.amazon.com/Gail-Ramshaw/e/B001JS8K68.

Don Saliers

Don E. Saliers is William R. Cannon Distinguished Professor of Theology and Worship, Emeritus at Emory University's Candler School of Theology, where he currently serves as theologian-in-residence. An accomplished musician, theologian, and scholar of liturgics, and a United Methodist pastor, Saliers has written numerous books and articles about worship and the arts that have influenced countless seminary students and pastors.

I interviewed Saliers at the annual meeting of the North American Academy of Liturgy in Houston on January 8, 2016, and recorded our conversation on video. More about the life and work of Don Saliers may be found on his faculty page at the Candler School of Theology, http://candler.emory.edu/faculty/profiles/saliers-don.html.

Melva Sampson

Melva L. Sampson is assistant professor of preaching and practical theology at Wake Forest University School of Divinity. A practical theologian and ordained minister, her research interests include Black preaching, women's embodiment, African heritage spiritual traditions, Black girls' ritual performance, and the relationship between digital proclamation and spiritual formation. She is the creator and curator of *Pink Robe Chronicles* and *Raising Womanish Girls*, both digital platforms used to elucidate the role of sacred memory and ritual in the collective healing of marginalized communities.

I interviewed Sampson online when she was in Atlanta and I was in Washington, DC, on January 5, 2016, and made a video recording of that conversation. More about Melva Sampson may be found on her faculty page on the website of the Wake Forest University School of Divinity at https://divinity.wfu.edu/academics/faculty/melva-l-sampson/.

Lisa Cole Smith

Lisa Cole Smith is an actor, director, pastor, and creative entrepreneur in the Washington, DC, area. She received her BFA in drama from Carnegie Mellon University in Pittsburgh and worked as a professional actor for many years before attending seminary and seeking a way to merge her calling as an artist and a person of faith. After receiving her MTS degree from the John Leland Center for Theological Studies in 2006, she founded an experimental church focused on art and artists called Convergence: A Creative Community of Faith.

I interviewed Smith in my office in Washington, DC,, on October 23, 2015, making a video recording of that conversation. Find out more about Lisa Cole Smith and Convergence at https://ourconvergence.org/.

Janet Walton

Janet Walton is professor of worship emerita at Union Theological Seminary in New York City. She is a past president of the North American Academy of Liturgy (1995–97), a Henry Luce Fellow in Theology and the Arts (1998), the recipient of a Henry Luce travel/research grant (1988), the 2003 recipient of the AAR Excellence in Teaching award, and the 2009 recipient of the Berakah Award, a lifetime award for distinctive work in worship given by the North American Academy of Liturgy.

I interviewed Walton at the annual meeting of the North American Academy of Liturgy in Houston on January 9, 2016, making a video recording of that conversation. In addition to her own teaching and service to the academy, her books, *Feminist Liturgy: A Matter of Justice* and *Art and Worship: A Vital Connection* have nourished countless students, pastors, and others interested the connections between feminism, worship, and the arts.

Index